**DO NOT REMOVE
CARDS FROM POCKET**

ALLEN COUNTY PUBLIC LIBRARY

FORT WAYNE, INDIANA 46802

You may return this book to any agency, branch,
or bookmobile of the Allen County Public Library.

DEMCO

SPECIAL EDUCATION SERIES

Winifred Anderson is a teacher and director of the Parent Educational Advocacy Training Center (PEATC).

Stephen Chitwood is a college professor, an attorney, and the father of a disabled child.

Deidre Hayden is a parent training specialist and the program coordinator for PEATC.

Winifred Anderson
Stephen Chitwood
Deidre Hayden

A Guide for Parents
and Teachers

NEGOTIATING THE SPECIAL EDUCATION MAZE

A SPECTRUM BOOK

Prentice-Hall, Inc., Englewood Cliffs, New Jersey 07632

Library of Congress Cataloging in Publication Data

Anderson, Winifred.
   Negotiating the special education maze.

   (Special education series)
   "A Spectrum Book."
   Includes bibliographical references and
index.
    1. Handicapped children—Education—United
States.   2. Handicapped children—Civil rights—
United States.   3. Home and school—United
States.   I. Chitwood, Stephen.   II. Hayden,
Deidre.   III. Series.
LC4031.A66   1982   371.9'0973   82–11222
ISBN 0-13-611129-7
ISBN 0-13-611111-4 [PBK.]

This Spectrum Book
can be made available to businesses and organizations
at a special discount when ordered in large quantities.
For more information, contact: Prentice-Hall, Inc.,
General Book Marketing, Special Sales Division,
Englewood Cliffs, New Jersey 07632

ISBN 0-13-611129-7
ISBN 0-13-611111-4 {PBK.}

A SPECTRUM BOOK

Printed in the United States of America

1 2 3 4 5 6 7 8 9 10

Editorial/production supervision by Alberta Boddy
Interior art by Jamie Ruppmann
Chapter opening layouts by Maria Carella
Manufacturing buyer: Cathie Lenard

Prentice-Hall International, Inc., *London*
Prentice-Hall of Australia Pty., Limited, *Sydney*
Prentice-Hall of Canada, Ltd., *Toronto*
Prentice-Hall of India Private, Limited, *New Delhi*
Prentice-Hall of Japan, Inc., *Tokyo*
Prentice-Hall of Southeast Asia Pte., Ltd., *Singapore*
Whitehall Books, Limited, *Wellington, New Zealand*

To Danny Chitwood

Contents

Preface

You care about your child, or you would not have picked up this book. You are motivated to help your child receive appropriate educational services or you would not be reading these pages. What you may feel you lack are skills and knowledge necessary to channel your caring and motivation into *actions* to *help* your child—the skills and knowledge to become an effective educational advocate. The purpose of this book is to help you become such an advocate. As your child's first and best educational advocate, you will assist the schoolteachers and administrators in designing special education services to meet your child's individual needs—to build on his or her particular strengths in order to bring about maximum change in those problems or limitations caused by a disability. Educators in the schools alone cannot ensure that your child will receive the educational program needed. Only parents—concerned, knowledgeable, and active parents—can guarantee the programs and services to which their children are entitled.

But how do you find your way through the complex and confusing procedures, meetings, and documents you are likely to encounter as you advocate for your child in the school system? *Negotiating the Special Education Maze* is a guide for parents whose school-aged children have disabilities requiring special education services. The book provides *directions and instructions* on how to unravel and master bewildering procedures used by the school systems for identifying and educating children with special learning needs. You will find *exercises and forms* to help you systematically and effectively share your unique knowledge of your child with educators. *Definitions and explanations* bring order and meaning to confusing terms you are apt to come across in reading psychological and educational evaluations, in eligibility or placement meetings, in writing the Individualized Education Program (IEP), and in a due process appeal. *Checklists* offer you alternative activities as you make decisions and prepare to participate as an educational advocate in your child's behalf. This book provides a step-by-step method for planning, securing, and overseeing your child's special education program.

From experiences as trainers of parent advocates, as educational and legal advocates, as educators and as parents, we have endeavored to write a practical guide based on methods proven effective in obtaining appropriate special education services for children. For many years these efforts have been supported by contributions of many people. In particular we express thanks to Virginia Houston, who read, edited, discussed, and developed many portions of the book; to Carolyn Beckett, the first person to use the manuscript as background material for teaching parents the skills of educational advocacy; to Michael Woodard, who assisted originally in the design of the parent training course in educational advocacy and who developed "Action-Steps for Evaluation" found in Chapter 3; to Virginia Maloney, consultant to schools and to parents, who developed and delivered a parent workshop, including the checklist for "Assessing a Learning Environment" in Chapter 6; to Susan Tolchin, herself an author, who provided thoughtful editorial comment; to Maryann McDermott, Joseph Clair, and Joseph Gilmore, who assisted us as project officers from the Office of Special Education; and to Judy Hutchinson, who willingly and cheerfully took pages she had carefully typed, then retyped them when we changed our minds. In addition, we express admiration and appreciation to those parents and professionals who have formed teams to teach the process of educational advocacy to other parents in communities throughout Virginia and other states. These team members used this book to inform and guide their work with parent groups and have provided us valuable comment as we prepared for final publication. Finally, to the hundreds of parents who participated in our training courses in educational advocacy, we say thank you for teaching us as you shared common and unique experiences with us.

NEGOTIATING
THE SPECIAL
EDUCATION MAZE

Introduction

Parents of special children throughout the nation are perplexed. For years school personnel have told them, "If only we could get the parents involved . . . ." But actions and words are often not the same. The experience of the Jacksons reflects this contradiction.

Like other conscientious parents, Mr. and Mrs. Jackson attended Parent-Teacher Association meetings, met with teachers at all scheduled conferences, sent notes to school persons discussing mutual concerns, volunteered for field trips and other classroom activities, and served on school-related committees in their community. Yet when their son Roger was referred by his classroom teacher to the special education screening committee of his school, Mr. and Mrs. Jackson immediately felt isolated and bewildered. They wanted to cooperate with school specialists to assess Roger's educational needs; so they gave permission to have Roger tested. What else could they do?

When their son's assessment was concluded, they attended the evaluation team meeting to learn the results. At the meeting educational specialists and school administrators talked of "scaled scores," "projective tests," "Bender-

Chapter 1

Charting
Your Course

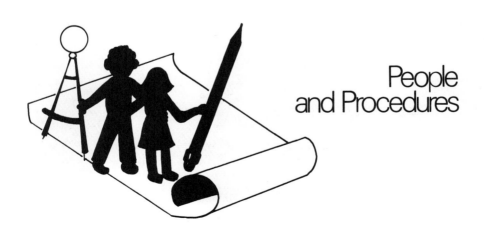

People
and Procedures

When parents are asked to read the list of feelings on the next page and to check the ones they experienced during a meeting with school personnel, the words they most often check include:

inadequate hopeful tentative challenged anxious

exhausted fearful confused worried

intimidated

For the most part these feelings tend to inhibit communication and to restrict participation.

Gestalt," "full-scale I.Q.," "WISC-R," and on and on. Mr. and Mrs. Jackson felt excluded, completely lost in the acronyms and rhetoric of "educationese." When they asked for clarification, the answers did little to alleviate their confusion. In this group of "specialists," they felt their opinions had little recognized value.

As the evaluation team members talked of "attentional deficits," "visual perception," "auditory acuity," and "maladaptive behavior," the Jacksons wondered where their lively, dark-haired, brown-eyed little boy fit into the picture. Certainly Roger had problems. But he was more than a bundle of negative behavior and problems dressed up in educational and psychological jargon. How could they get these people to see Roger in all his complexity? How could they affect the actions these school officials would take relating to their son? How could they handle their increasing sense of being railroaded into prepackaged decisions made by the "experts"—special education teachers, educational specialists, psychologists, and administrators?

Many thought the answers to these questions were finally provided when, in 1975, President Ford signed into law Public Law 94-142, the Education for All Handicapped Children Act. The legislation mandated the role of parents as equal partners in formulating educational decisions for their handicapped children. As the legislation has unfolded over the years, events have begun to obscure the law's original intent and to bring into question whether the realization of the law may ever occur.

To illustrate: School personnel complain of being overburdened with paperwork, scheduling problems, overdemanding parents, and lack of money. Parents, hoping to realize the promise of cooperation with the schools for their child's well-being, feel like unwelcome intruders if their participation is more than passive acceptance of what the school people prescribe. The complicated process of referral, assessment, and selection of services too often has parents caught in the posture either of compliant recipient or hostile critic. What they have heard over the years from school systems urging more parent involvement now echoes with the wish that parents go away and leave the job of education to the educators.

Educational advocacy addresses this dilemma. An advocate is one who stands and speaks in behalf of another person or group of persons in order to bring about change. Advocates have emerged into positions of increasing prominence in the last decade. There are those like Ralph Nader who are consumer advocates, working to influence regulatory agencies to bring about change in the quality of products we purchase. Political advocates seek to bring about social and economic change through state and national legislatures. Legal advocates use our court system to bring about change in the interpretation of laws that affect our lives.

The Education for All Handicapped Children Act empowers parents to become *educational advocates* for their children. An educational advocate is one who speaks knowledgeably for the educational needs of another person. You, the parents, are the ones who know your child best. It is you who can speak most effectively in his or her behalf in order to obtain the free, appropriate public education promised by law. This book was written to assist you in your role as educational advocate—to help you gain the knowledge required to be an effective educational planner for your child, to assist you in presenting your child in the best possible way, to suggest how to cope with your feelings, and to guide you through the often complex maze of special education.

Many school systems and interest groups have written manuals to assist parents and teachers. Most of these books or pamphlets describe the legal requirements for special education, the procedures of the school system, characteristics of handicapping conditions, and regulations prescribed by the state and local school systems. They are limited in that they all stress what the *school system* knows—its rules and regulations—and neglect the parent and the child. Perhaps this explains why you have not found them particularly helpful.

This book is different. It begins with what you know better than anyone— *your own child.* This is a practical step-by-step guide based upon the experience of several hundred families as they have worked to secure good special education services for their children. *Negotiating the Special Education Maze: A Guide for Parents and Teachers* is the outgrowth of work and learning by parents who have participated in a parent training course sponsored by the Parent Educational Advocacy Training Center in Alexandria, Virginia. Parents from many school divisions in Virginia and other states have attended a fifteen-hour course to increase their knowledge of school systems' procedures, to learn skills in organizing and presenting observations of their children, and to become more assertive and effective in their role as educational advocates for their children. The understanding those parents have gained of the value of active participation in educational planning is shared with you; indeed, their experience is the basis for this study guide.

If you follow the instructions well, this book should provide sufficient training in educational advocacy. You also can build on this text to start your own course in parent advocacy for your community. This involves organizing a group of parents, and locating someone trained to be a leader of the course. Involved parents can then work through these steps with help from others, enabling them not only to communicate about their child more clearly and effectively, but also to learn from others' experiences in working with school systems. This book can point the way toward additional sources of assistance—books, resource groups, and other training courses.

Whether you study alone or with a group, this manual is written with you, the parents, in mind. Some of you have spent many years working to get appropriate school services for your children. Others are just embarking on the road through the special education maze. The authors hope this road map will assist you in making an efficient journey, where your own personal resources are used and appreciated. At the end you should find your special child making progress, because you and school personnel are partners in his well-being.

List of Feelings That Persons Have but Often Fail to Identify

Abandoned	Determined	Helpless	Obsessed	Strangled
Adamant	Different	High	Odd	Stuffed
Adequate	Diffident	Homesick	Opposed	Stunned
Affectionate	Diminished	Honored	Outraged	Stupefied
Agonized	Discontented	Hopeful	Overwhelmed	Stupid
Almighty	Disturbed	Horrible		Suffering
Ambivalent	Divided	Hurt	Pain	Sure
Angry	Dominated	Hysterical	Panicked	Suspicious
Annoyed	Dubious		Parsimonious	Sympathetic
Anxious		Ignored	Peaceful	
Apathetic	Eager	Inadequate	Persecuted	Taciturn
Astounded	Ecstatic	Immortal	Petrified	Talkative
Awed	Electrified	Infatuated	Pitying	Tempted
	Empty	Infuriated	Pleasant	Tenacious
Bad	Enchanted	Inspired	Pleased	Tenuous
Beautiful	Energetic	Intimidated	Precarious	Tense
Betrayed	Enervated	Isolated	Prim	Tentative
Bitter	Enjoyed		Prissy	Terrible
Blissful	Enraged	Jealous	Proud	Terrified
Bold	Envious	Joyous		Threatened
Bored	Evil	Jumpy	Quarrelsome	Tired
Brave	Exasperated		Queer	Troubled
Burdened	Excited	Keen		Truculent
	Exhausted	Kind	Rapture	
Calm		Kinky	Refreshed	Ugly
Capable	Fascinated	Knowledgable	Rejected	Uneasy
Captivated	Fawning		Relaxed	Unsettled
Challenged	Fearful	Laconic	Relieved	Unsure
Charmed	Flustered	Lazy	Remorse	
Cheated	Foolish	Lecherous	Restless	Vehement
Cheerful	Frantic	Left out	Reverent	Violent
Childish	Frustrated	Licentious	Rewarded	Vital
Clever	Frightened	Lonely	Righteous	Vivacious
Combative	Free	Longing		Vulnerable
Competitive	Full	Loving	Sad	
Condemned	Furious	Low	Sated	Weepy
Confident			Satisfied	Wicked
Confused	Gay	Mad	Scared	Wonderful
Conspicuous	Glad	Maudlin	Screwed up	Worried
Contented	Good	Mean	Servile	
Contrite	Gratified	Melancholy	Settled	Zany
Cruel	Greedy	Miserable	Sexy	Zesty
Crushed	Grief	Mystical	Shocked	
Culpable	Groovy		Silly	
	Guilty	Naughty	Skeptical	
Deceitful	Gullible	Nervous	Sneaky	
Defeated		Nice	Solemn	
Delighted	Happy	Niggardly	Sorrowful	
Desirous	Hateful	Nutty	Spiteful	
Despair	Heavenly		Startled	
Destructive	Helpful	Obnoxious	Stingy	

On the other hand, when a group of teachers was asked to use the same list of words and to reflect on a recent teacher-parent conference, they checked:

SURE   CALM

CAPABLE   HELPFUL

CONFIDENT   ADEQUATE

ENERGETIC   KNOWLEDGEABLE

What makes the difference? As parents going into school meetings, you are moving into territory where the people you meet use a language and a body of knowledge you may not understand completely. The school people are living with routines and regulations unfamiliar to you, familiar to them. All people carry some remnants of their own school experience into school buildings—some good and some not so good. Perceptions of school officials and your own school experiences may cause you to question your ability to say the right thing at the right time and to convey your cares, hopes, and opinions about your child's best interests and needs.

What helps parents overcome their feelings of anxiety, confusion, and incompetence? The more knowledge you have of the educational planning process and of the people who participate in that process, the more comfortable you will become in your role as advocate for your child. As you gain skills in presenting your view of your child to the school people, negative feelings like inadequacy and incompetence will diminish, allowing you to be a more effective partner in the educational planning process. This guidebook will help you gain the knowledge and skills you need.

SUSIE MARTIN: A CASE STUDY

During Susie's year in kindergarten, her mother, Mrs. Martin, felt concern when other children in the class were better able than Susie to do many of the pencil and paper tasks given to them. Susie's crayon pictures continued to be mainly scribbles. Toward the end of the school year she was still unable to copy the letters in her name. Susie was restless. During group and story time she was apt to jump up and move about the room, playing with objects on other children's desks or in the storage cabinets. When her teacher called her back to the group she would roll around the floor, twisting her hair, apparently off in her own world. She didn't listen to the story.

For the first months of the school year, the teacher said Susie would soon learn the expectations in the classroom and would improve in her skills and her behavior. Mr. and Mrs. Martin continued to worry, but listened to the teacher's suggestions. Finally, late in the year, the kindergarten teacher recommended that Susie be tested by the school's psychologist. This testing would help to determine whether or not she needed special education during the coming school year. Mr. and Mrs. Martin readily consented to the testing. They felt relieved that something was finally being done to see if Susie had a learning problem.

Since most of the school psychologists were away during the summer, testing for Susie had to be postponed until early in September. Reluctantly, the Martins waited. When September came, the testing began. But in the meantime Susie was having an even more difficult time in the first grade. She noticed that other children were easily doing many things she couldn't do. Her behavior both at school and at home was often unacceptable. The Martins were angry that the school system was not giving Susie the special help they were now sure she needed. The school administrators defended themselves by invoking the regulations they were required to follow before declaring a child eligible for special education. Everyone was frustrated and angry.

What kind of help eases such a situation? Parents and school systems each have a planning cycle for children with special needs. Understanding the two cycles and how they should work together can often help resolve the disagreement. The cycles look like this:

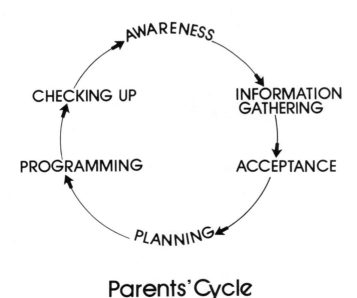

Parents' Cycle

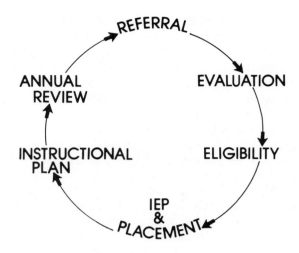

School System's Cycle

The Martins' *awareness* of problems in Susie's school life came early in her kindergarten year. They began to *gather information* that might help them to understand and to help Susie. They talked to their pediatrician, observed other children Susie's age, read some books on child development and learning problems, and talked frequently with the kindergarten teacher. On the basis of all the facts they observed about Susie and the knowledge they gained through other sources, they came to an *acceptance* of their original hunch that Susie did indeed

have some problems needing special education at school. They talked again with the school principal and kindergarten teacher, hoping that *planning* for Susie's special needs would begin. They were ready early in the school year for Susie to have special education *programming*.

The school system, on the other hand, was reluctant so early in a child's school life to refer her for special services. The kindergarten teacher had a "wait and see" attitude. Toward the end of the school year, though, the teacher activated the school system's planning cycle. She made a *referral* to the school psychologist for testing. The *evaluation* process of psychological, educational, and other testing involved the teacher, the school psychologist, the school health service, and a social worker. All of these professionals were a part of the required multidisciplinary team, who worked to understand Susie and the problems she was having. This evaluation process, interrupted by summer vacation, was completed in the fall. The results of the series of tests were presented to the special education department. The assessment team recommended Susie's *eligibility* for special services. The Martins were invited to participate in the meeting that summarized the findings of the evaluation and made the determination of her eligibility for special education. Following the eligibility decision, the Martins and the school personnel, including a special education teacher, met together to plan for Susie's needs in an *individualized education program* and *placement* meeting. Only at this time were the parents' planning cycle and the school system's planning cycle synchronized.

Finally, some of the tension and frustration was alleviated. The Martins had been ready for Susie to receive special education *instruction* several months before the school system had completed the required cycle of referral, evaluation, eligibility, Individualized Education Program (IEP), and placement. Once the cycles meshed, cooperative planning for Susie's well-being became possible. Subsequently, Susie began to have a more successful time in school.

In contrast to Susie Martin's case, conflicts may arise between parents and school systems when school people have continual concerns about a child's performance in school. They recommend a formal evaluation in order to understand the child's problems. But parents are certain that there is no problem. They feel that their child's maturation will naturally take care of the difficulties, and are therefore unwilling to give the required permission for the school evaluation to proceed. In this instance the school is ahead of the parents in the cycle. While the parents are barely, or not at all, in the awareness phase, the school system is ready for the next step, evaluation. In this situation the synchronization necessary for collaborative planning is not yet present.

These planning cycles, both for parents and for school people, most often are recurring cycles. During the *checking up* and *annual review,* a need for change is sometimes apparent. Any time there is a change, or a proposed change in a child's school program, both cycles begin anew.

For you, the parents of a child who may need special education, a better understanding of the school system's cycle can help to clarify your participation as educational advocates. The school system's cycle is described in the rules and regulations published by the school system in your community. The following two activities will help you understand how your school's special education process works. The understanding you gain will help to change some of your feelings of inadequacy and uncertainty into ones of competency.

Every school system in the country has a set of regulations governing special education. The complexity of the regulations will vary, however, from locality to locality. Some large school systems have documents of a hundred or more pages outlining their procedures. Other school systems have no more than a page or two of mimeographed regulations. The first part of Activity #1 is to contact your school superintendent, director of special education, or special education advisory committee and ask for a copy of your local school system's procedures and regulations for special education. These are available to all citizens. A copy of your school system's regulations will help you gain confidence in your ability to be an advocate for your child—you, as well as the school people, will know the procedures!

When the local school system wrote their procedural guidelines, they had to follow the regulations of their state division of special education. So a second part of Activity #1 is to write your state director of special education and ask for a copy of the state regulations governing special education. Obtaining state regulations is especially important for parents whose children are served in school systems whose regulations are not highly structured and developed. Many local school systems simply follow what the state has written with no elaboration. Appendix A has a list of addresses of all divisions of special education in the United States and territories. Again, because you are a citizen and because special education regulations are public documents, you should have easy access to this information. At the very least, these documents should be available in either your public library or a public school library. If you have trouble locating the regulations, someone in the office of your state legislator can help you.

You now have the regulations as developed by your local school system and/or your state department of education. You are ready for Activity #2.

ACTIVITY #2:
KEY PEOPLE

For every phase of the educational planning process there are key individuals involved. By making your own personal directory of school officials, including names, addresses, and telephone numbers, you will clarify the roles of certain individuals in the educational planning process, and you will save time in identifying them when you need their assistance. On the next page you will find an example of a Key People Chart.

As you read the regulations from your locality, you will most likely find terminology and names of key positions varying from the ones in the following example. Generally the terminology and names of key positions will be similar, since state and local regulations must conform to the federal regulations governing the Education for All Handicapped Children Act, PL 94-142.* In Appendix B you will find a chart showing several states' processes for educational planning. You may find these helpful as a model for developing an understanding of the process for your school system with terminology used by your state and locality.

You have obtained the rules and regulations describing and guiding the special education process in your school system. You have identified the key people with whom you must work in securing appropriate services for your child. You are ready, at this time, to begin developing the picture and understanding of your child you wish to convey in school meetings. But what information do you, as parents, possess that could possibly be helpful in outlining the special educational needs and programs of your child? The following chapter clearly illustrates the unique knowledge parents have of their children, the importance of that knowledge for educational planning, and how parents may develop and provide that critical information to school officials.

---

*"Rules and Regulations," Department of Health, Education and Welfare, Office of Education, Education of Handicapped Children, Implementation of Part B of the Education of the Handicapped Act, Federal Register 42:163, 23 August 1979.

EDUCATIONAL PLANNING PROCESS

KEY PEOPLE

SCHOOL JURISDICTION _Alexandria, Virginia_

Name	Address	Telephone

I. REFERRAL

Louise Fischer
Referring person _223 Maple Place_ _263-8192_

Eileen Collins
Local School Principal _Westbriar Elem. School_ _691-4261_

II. LOCAL SCHOOL SCREENING COMMITTEE

Eileen Collins
*Principal or designee
(chairperson) " "

Louise Fischer
*Referring person

Anna Chase
*Teacher(s)/Specialist(s)
as appropriate _807-16th Street_ (w) 691-4261
(h) 389-3227

Fred Duncan
Friend of supporting person _9 Spring Garden_ _584-2963_

III. EVALUATION TEAM (MULTIDISCIPLINARY)

Katy Lothian, psychologist
Evaluation Team Coordinator _Westbriar Elementary_ _691-4261_

"   "   "
Case Manager

Anna Chase
*Teacher(s)/Specialist(s)
with knowledge of sus-
pected disability)

Dr. Roger Hackett
Independent Evaluator
(when appropriate) _7 Oleander Road_ _263-2651_

IV. ELIGIBILITY COMMITTEE

Dr. Martin Robinson
*Administrator of Special
Education Program or
designee

North Central Administration Building   691-9200 ext. 34

Katy Lothian
*Evaluation Team Member(s)
(presents evaluation
findings)

Westbriar Elementary   691-4261

Dr. Joanne Wilson
Appropriate Special Edu-
cation Administrators

North Cent. Admin. Bldg   691-9200 ext. 48

Nancy Henderson
Other professional staff

"   " ext. 52

Fred Duncan
Friend or supporting
person

V. INDIVIDUALIZED EDUCATION PROGRAM MEETING

Eileen Collins, principal
*School division repre-
sentative qualified to
provide or supervise
Special Education Services

Westbriar Elem.   691-4261

Anna Chase
*Teacher

"   389-3227

Child, if appropriate

Fred Duncan
Friend or supporting
person

584-2963

VI. INDIVIDUALIZED EDUCATION PROGRAM ANNUAL REVIEW

     Same team as in the IEP Meeting

*Persons required by Regulations and Administrative Requirements
for the Operation of Special Education Programs in Virginia,
June 23, 1978.

Chapter 2

You
and Your Child

Strengthening Exercises for the Journey

PREPARING FOR THE JOURNEY
THROUGH THE MAZE

In planning your journey through the maze, there are a number of activities, or exercises, you can do to prepare yourself. Although you can wend your way through the maze without completing the exercises, your trip will be more productive—you will be less likely to go up "blind alleys"—if you complete some Strengthening Exercises. One exercise prepares you for the next; the exercises build upon each other.

Where do you begin your trip through the special education maze? You begin by taking a look at the central figure in the whole planning process—your child.

To assist you in focusing on your child, a "Learning Style Questionnaire," Strengthening Exercise #1, follows. Take some time right now to write your responses to the five questions. An example of Strengthening Exercise #1 completed by Sara's parents can be found on the following page.

1. List three things your child has recently learned or accomplished.

   1)

   2)

   3)

   Choose one of the items in question #1. What about your child helped him learn this?

3. Think of three things your child is working to learn now.

   1)

   2)

   3)

4. Choose one of the items in question #3 that your child is having trouble learning. What is causing him trouble?

5. What one thing would you like your child to learn within the next six months?

STRENGTHENING EXERCISE #1. Learning Style Questionnaire.

Keep this information, because it is necessary for your next steps as you proceed through the special education maze. Strengthening Exercise #1 provides the first step to help you obtain specific information about your child, and to discover the keys that make it easier for him or her to learn.

OBSERVING YOUR CHILD IN A SYSTEMATIC WAY

Sometimes parents experience difficulties in answering the questions in Strengthening Exercise #1. You have much knowledge about your child, but the knowledge is often felt in a more general sense than in the specific terms needed to answer these questions. Because you are absorbed in the routine of everyday living, you are constantly gathering information about your child, automatically. Perhaps you do not realize how much you do know!

In order to convey a personal knowledge of your child to the school people—those who are accustomed to dealing with test scores, specific behaviors, goals, and objectives—it is important to collect your own facts. Your innate feel-

1. List three things your child has recently learned or accomplished.

    1) *Sara writes short poems to her friends on birthday and get well cards*

    2) *She completes chores such as making beds and taking dishes to the kitchen*

    3) *She draws pictures that are more recognizable*

    4) *She finishes a short book she starts*

2. Choose one of the items in question #1. What about your child helped him learn this?
    She enjoys making home chore charts and checking off progress as she completes the chores

3. Think of three things your child is working to learn now.

    1) *Sara is learning the music notes for piano playing*

    2) *to read a short book, organize her thoughts and give an oral book report*

    3) *to use her time in the morning without Mom's prodding her*

4. Choose one of the items in question #3 that your child is having trouble learning. What is causing him trouble?
    day dreaming, distractions in her bedroom such as toys

5. What one thing would you like your child to learn within the next six months?
    I would like for Sara to get herself completely ready for school each morning without my having to prod or help her.

ings about your child need to be changed from generalized impressions and concerns into specific, documented observations. With written, concrete facts, you will be prepared to contribute to the planning of your child's education program.

One way to do this is actually to observe your child. "Observe!" you say. "When? How?" You think of the days you barely have enough time and energy to brush your teeth before turning in for the night. But observations can be made. The information-gathering process is a vital part of becoming an effective educational advocate.

Following are some suggestions to help you develop and sharpen your observation skills.

ONE STEP BACKWARD— THREE STEPS FORWARD

STEP BACK   Suspend for a brief time (five minutes) your normal role in family life. Step back from your family situation to put some distance between you and your child. By not intervening where you normally would, you may see your child and his abilities in a new light.

START FRESH   Current eyewitness reports supply better data than do events of the past. Although the past is important in describing your child's development, school personnel are interested in what he can do *now*. Start fresh, also, in how you view your own child. Try to be open to new aspects you may have overlooked before. Be alert yourself, as the observer. A tired or preoccupied observer does not record what is happening as accurately as one who is concentrating on the matter at hand.

GET FOCUSED   Decide upon a specific behavior to observe. You can plan your observation to include various factors: who will be with your child, as well as where and when you will observe him. For example, Sara's parents decided to gather information about the development of Sara's use of her hands. They planned to observe Sara playing with her friend, working at school, and setting the dinner table at home. During each of those times, they recorded specific information relevant to Sara's fine motor skills. On pages 21 and 22 you will find examples of people, places, and activities you might include as you plan to observe your child.

GO WITH THE FLOW   As you watch your child's activities, record what you see actually happening, not your interpretations of your child's actions. For instance, Sara's parents observed her at school, as she practiced tracing shapes and designs. They noted the way she grasped her pencil, the complexity of the design she was tracing, and whether she was able to repeat the design consistently.

Recording detailed, factual information is easier if a short time is spent observing—perhaps ten minutes or less. Observing your child frequently for short periods will help you in your task of recording facts—exactly what happens. You can go back later, review your collection of observations, and interpret the data.

Now! Actually observe your child, with a specific behavior or skill in mind. Step back from your usual role as Mom or Dad, write down what occurs, and save interpretations for later.

GUIDELINES
FOR PLANNING AN OBSERVATION

A. *Who,* if anybody, will be interacting with your child?

1. parent	6. relative(s)
2. brothers or sisters	7. stranger(s)
3. best friend	8. tutor
4. several friends	9. teacher
5. unfamiliar children	10. professional(s)

B. *Where* will the observation happen—in what setting?
   1. Home
      a. your child's room
      b. TV room
      c. dining room
      d. backyard
      e. homework space
   2. Neighborhood
      a. neighbor's house
      b. friend's house
      c. around the block
      d. playground
      e. special places: woods, fields, water
   3. Family Events
      a. picnics
      b. car trips
      c. weddings
      d. visits to relatives
   4. Small Crowds
      a. eating out
      b. shopping
      c. museums
      d. pet stores
      e. parties
   5. Big Crowds
      a. ballgames
      b. zoo
      c. riding the bus
   6. School
      a. classroom
      b. therapy session
      c. field trip
      d. playground
      e. evaluations

C. *When* will the observation occur in your child's day?
   1. mealtime
   2. bedtime
   3. good time of day
   4. bad time of day
   5. worktime
   6. playtime
   7. stress time
   8. sick time

D. *What* will you be looking at in the observation?
   Here is a sample of information parents can seek and obtain through observation. Some are quite specific and others are more general and complicated.
   1. How does my child handle a flight of stairs?
   2. How does my child play with small toys like Lego, Litebrite, beads, and computer games?
   3. How does my child hold a pencil?
   4. How does my child organize his or her toys like dolls, soldiers, cars, blocks, and baseball cards?
   5. How does my child handle unfamiliar situations?
   6. How does my child deal with frustration?
   7. How does my child participate in group games?
   8. How does my child make friends?
   9. How does my child solve problems with friends?
   10. What activities does my child enjoy the most?
   11. In what circumstances is my child able to study best?
   12. When is my child's attention span longest? shortest?
   13. How do changes in my child's routine affect him?
   14. What distracts my child from doing her homework?

The information you gather by observing your child will add to the specific data necessary in planning an educational program to meet your child's unique needs. Strengthening Exercise #2, Parents' Observation Record, provides you with a sample form to assist you in keeping a log of your observations. An example of the Parents' Observation Record completed by Sara's parents is found on page 24.

OBSERVER_____DATE OF OBSERVATION_____

BEGINNING TIME OF OBSERV._____ENDING TIME_____

WHO IS OBSERVED_____

WHERE_____WHEN_____

WHAT WAS THE FOCUS OF THE OBSERVATION:_____

_____

WHY WAS THIS FOCUS CHOSEN:_____

_____

WHAT OCCURRED DURING OBSERVATION	REFLECTIONS ON OBSERVATION

STRENGTHENING EXERCISE #2. Parents' Observation Record.

After you collect several observation records, you can compare and contrast them, looking for trends and consistencies or inconsistencies in your child's behavior. Organizing your observations is a vital part of the information-gathering phase to prepare you to meet with school personnel.

Here are some examples of behaviors parents recorded in their observations in Strengthening Exercises #1 and #2.

- Jason does homework best in a quiet, uncrowded place.
- Fred can recite the alphabet.
- May Lin can put two words together to speak in phrases.
- Virginia has learned to catch herself with her arms as she falls.
- Orin catches and throws a large ball.
- Enrico can write a short paragraph with the ideas in proper sequence.

- Jamie puts on her shoes and socks by herself.
- Tyrone shares his toys with Sandra.
- Dee eats with a spoon.
- Steve writes capital and lower-case letters in cursive.
- Shantell learns best when she works with one or two good friends.
- Denise can copy a pattern of colored beads strung together.
- Carolyn shows off her school work with pride and excitement.
- Ellen understands thirty-two words signed in manual communication.

PARENTS' OBSERVATION RECORD

OBSERVER _Gina_   DATE OF OBSERVATION _Oct. 29_

BEGINNING TIME OF OBSERV. _7 15 Am_ ENDING TIME _7 20 Am_

WHO OBSERVED _Sara_

WHERE _Sara's bedroom_   WHEN _getting ready for school_

WHAT WAS THE FOCUS OF THE OBSERVATION: _to watch and_
understand Sara's morning patterns

WHY WAS THIS FOCUS CHOSEN: _family uproar over Sara's_
dawdling

WHAT OCCURRED DURING OBSERVATION	REFLECTIONS ON OBSERVATION
Gets out of bed when called	Sister's call puts additional stress
Picks up book to read	
Looks at clock	Room is too cluttered
Hears sister call impatiently	She needs a written morning schedule to follow
Puts book down, walks to dresser	
Picks up doll and plays with doll's shoes	Put a schedule on her bulletin board ??

In order to use these observations to a child's best advantage—and that's what educational advocacy is all about—parents need to take these bits and pieces of observed behavior and organize them to coincide with developmental categories used by school personnel. Organizing the observation records into general areas of child development will help you think about and discuss your child in ways similar to those of educators.

The preceding list of behaviors parents have observed can be organized into seven broad developmental areas:

movement
communications
social relationships
self concept/independence skills
perception/senses
thinking skills
learning style

Now, you ask, are these the categories child development specialist or schoolteachers use? In fact, other common terminology might have included such terms as cognition, self-help, gross motor, expressive language, auditory or visual perception—and on and on and on. There are many classification systems, but basically they are the same. They serve to structure observations about human growth and development. There are some who suggest parents learn the terminology of physicians, educators, therapists, and other specialists. This guidebook assumes the viewpoint that *your* language about your child is the best language. So, for purposes of educational advocacy in this book, very generalized developmental categories are suggested. They should fit with very little squeezing, translation, or interpretation into the categories others are using.

DEFINITIONS

MOVEMENT   The ability to use muscles and the body to accomplish certain objectives such as walking, jumping, balancing, holding objects, rolling, moving oneself around objects, writing, etc.

COMMUNICATIONS   The ability to understand and respond to language and to speak clearly and with meaning.

SOCIAL RELATIONSHIPS   The ability to relate intentionally to one or more persons.

SELF CONCEPT/INDEPENDENCE   The ability to distinguish oneself from others and to care for one's own needs.

PERCEPTION/SENSES   The ability to use eyes, ears, and senses of touch, smell, and taste to learn about one's environment.

THINKING SKILL   The ability to classify, to make associations, to understand similarities and differences, and to comprehend cause-and-effect relationships. The school skills of reading, arithmetic, spelling, and so forth can be placed in this category.

LEARNING STYLE   The unique ways in which one learns—those personality traits that contribute to success. This category includes paying attention, organizing, remembering, getting help, planning, and following through.

One of the most valuable contributions parents make to the educational planning process is describing their child's unique *learning style*. Think for a minute about the way *you* learn best. For example:

- Do you learn best by reading material and information?
- Maybe you understand things better when you have participated in group discussions.
- Are you someone who needs absolute quiet when you concentrate?
- Perhaps you like classical music as background to your thinking.
- Maybe you can concentrate longer if you are chewing gum and some of your excess energy is used that way.
- Do you need to draw pictures, diagrams, or charts to help you analyze a problem?

Thinking about how you learn can make you aware of your child's special ways of learning. There is no right or wrong way. A good learning environment for you may be quite different from that of your child. Be aware—be alert—to some of the unique aspects of the way your boy or girl learns. Share this information with those who are teaching him so they, too, can help to create the best setting for his needs.

The recorded observations on pages 23 and 24 parents have made of their children can be categorized into these developmental areas:

Movement:	Virginia
	Orin
	Steve
Communications:	May Lin
	Ellen

Social Relationships:	Tyrone
Independence/Self Concept:	Carolyn
	Dee
	Jamie
Perception/Senses:	Denise
Thinking Skills:	Enrico
	Fred
Learning Style:	Jason
	Shantell

But you might say Jamie's behavior of putting on her shoes and socks independently fits into the skill areas of *movement* and *thinking skills,* as well as *independence.* No behavior falls exclusively into one category or another. Jamie's movement skills are fine. Physically she is able to put on her shoes and socks. The emphasis she needs is developing her independence. Therefore her parents place "putting on shoes and socks" under *Independence/Self Concept.* Think about what developmental areas are particularly important to your child's growth at this time, and put your observations of his accomplishments into that category. Remember, there need not be only one "right" category.

Take the work you have done in the first two Strengthening Exercises and put each observation into an appropriate category in the following chart. Notice that Question #1 on the Learning Style Questionnaire provides information for the column *Can Do.* Question #3 on the Learning Style Questionnaire coincides with the second column, *Working On.* Question #5 corresponds with the column *To Accomplish in 6 Months.* Questions #2 and #4 give information about your child's *learning style.* These observations can be recorded in the bottom row of the chart.

On page 24 you will find an example of how Sara's parents organized their observations into the *framework.*

DEVELOPMENTAL ACHIEVEMENT CHART	Can Do	Working On	To Accomplish within 6 Months
MOVEMENT			
COMMUNICATIONS			
SOCIAL RELATIONSHIPS			
SELF-CONCEPT/ INDEPENDENCE			
SENSES/PERCEPTION			
THINKING SKILLS			
LEARNING STYLE			

STRENGTHENING EXERCISE #3. Developmental Achievement Chart.

DEVELOPMENTAL ACHIEVEMENT CHART

	Can Do	Working On	To Accomplish within 6 Months
MOVEMENT	Rides a bike, walks the balance beam. Writes cursive. Throws a ball.	Pedalling faster & pumping up hill for her bike & smaller and neater cursive. Catching a large ball.	To keep up with a group when bike riding. Write cursive on narrow line paper. Catch and throw accurately
COMMUNICATIONS	Makes her needs known in a vague way. Responds to simple directions	Using specific words - not "whatcha-ma-call-it." Following instructions without getting mixed up	To increase thinking of and saying the right words. Understand & follow through on more complex directions
SOCIAL RELATIONSHIPS	Be a part of a junior Girl Scout troop. Plays along side other girls, often younger children	Being an accepted and liked member of group - made adult help. Establishing close friendship with girl her own age	Participate in small group activity without adult hovering over. Stay/spend the night time with another girl
SELF-CONCEPT/ INDEPENDENCE	Gets dressed in morning if clothes are laid out & left. Answer telephone politely. Walks from bus stop alone - expects Mom to be waiting	Finding proper clothes - lay them out the night before. Listen to caller's name & message. Learning what to do if I'm late	Dress completely without reminders. Write complete telephone message. Decide what to do if I'm late & not waiting
SENSES/PERCEPTION	Sees music notes and identify middle C	Learning names of notes on music staff - beginning to find them on piano	Play simple tunes by reading the notes
THINKING SKILLS	Identifies coins & names them. Reads a short story - has a general idea if coherent when she finishes	Understanding the value of each coin. Pick out the main idea in a paragraph or story	Buy something with her allowance and count the change. Understand and tell the main idea in short story or chapter
LEARNING STYLE	Daydreams, distractable. Responds positively to praise. Needs a lot of direction for even simple activities	Structuring her own activities with charts	Be able to make her own charts and be responsible for following them

There are many times, places, and ways of collecting information about your child's growth and development. Here are some sources other parents have found useful—add your own to the lists:

people

Grandparents
Brothers, sisters
Scout leaders
Coaches
Neighbors

Playmates
Bus drivers
Teachers
Doctors

places

McDonald's
Family camping
Household chores
Carpools

Church
Grocery store
Scout troop
Swimming lessons

family
documents
& projects

Photo albums
Examples of school work
Coloring Easter eggs
Home movies
School and hospital records

Art projects
Tape recordings

Chapter 3

Ready? Go!
Referral and Evaluation

INTRODUCTION

You have now collected important information describing your child's educational and developmental achievements and learning style. But where does all this fit within the school system's special education planning process? How, and at what point, can you get school personnel to discuss with you your concerns and findings regarding your child's educational needs? How do you get the school system to evaluate your child more thoroughly? What information can you obtain about these evaluations and other matters contained in your child's official school records?

Chapter 1 briefly described the phases of the planning cycle school systems use in providing educational services for special-needs children. This chapter examines in detail two of these phases: *referral* and *evaluation*. Each phase is described in terms of its purposes, activities, and participants. More important, suggestions are made as to how you, as parents, can actively and positively participate in these phases. As you acquire a better understanding of these activities and how you can participate in them, you will move yet another step closer toward negotiating the special education maze.

IDENTIFYING SPECIAL-NEEDS CHILDREN: THE REFERRAL PHASE

Children who have educational or developmental problems frequently are observed by a number of adults; for example, parents, teachers, doctors, coaches. Not all of these persons, however, have opportunity to notify the schools of the need these children may have for special education services. Just who, then, can refer your child to be considered for special education?

The rules and regulations of both your local school system and your state division of special education will identify who may refer your child for special services and how that referral is to be made. Generally, parents, guardians, teachers, or other school officials can make these referrals. In some places, physicians, social workers, psychologists, or other professionals may be the referring person. If a child is entering a school for the first time and parents believe special education is needed, they may request that the child be considered for such assistance immediately. Or if teachers and counselors notice a child is having problems in school, they may make a referral.

When a child is thought to need special education, the usual first procedure is a written referral to a committee within his local school. The school to which the referral is made is the one the child is attending or would attend if he were in a public school. The committee appointed to consider special education referrals is composed of: (1) the principal or someone designated by the principal; (2) the person who referred the child, if that person is from the school system; and (3) teachers or other specialists who have particular knowledge of the problems the child seems to be experiencing.

In many school jurisdictions this initial committee is called the local school screening committee. The major objective of the committee is to determine whether a child's problem is severe enough to require further formal evaluation by the school psychologist and other specialists. The decision of the committee is often required to be made in writing and to include the information leading to the committee's conclusions. The exact number of days in which the committee must act is usually set forth in your school's rules and regulations. If the committee believes further evaluation of your child is required, the necessary recommendation is sent to the school's special education administrator.

At this stage of the process parents are often unaware that their child has even been referred to the local school screening committee. When referrals are made by teachers or other school personnel, parents frequently are not notified of such actions—nor is such notification required in many states. Since the screening committee review may recommend "no action," schools often feel they are doing parents a favor by not notifying them, thus avoiding unnecessary alarm. Furthermore, since no tests or other special evaluations are required of your child prior to this meeting, the schools have no legal duty to inform you of these initial referral meetings.

In those instances where you, the parent, have referred your child for initial screening, you should request that the local screening committee advise you of the time when they will meet and allow you to participate in that meeting. While the committee may not be required to allow your participation, they usually are agreeable to such participation when asked. In preparation for this meeting, you should observe your child as described in Chapter 2 and develop a presentation of those findings and any other matters you believe would assist the local screening committee in its consideration of your child.

At this meeting the screening committee will both review a child's records and other relevant material and decide whether to recommend further evaluation. If you attend the screening meeting, you should ask to participate in the discussion leading to that decision. Once again, the regulations will probably not require the committee to allow your participation in their final discussion and decision-making. Nevertheless, they often will let you remain for the discussion and final decision, if you request it. So go ahead and ask.

TAKING A LOOK: THE EVALUATION PROCESS

If parents have not been part of the screening committee's activities, they may first learn that their child is being considered for special educational services upon receipt of a letter from the school requesting permission to evaluate their child. Under federal and state laws, school systems must notify parents of their wish to evaluate their children for purposes of receiving special education services. Further, the parents' permission must be granted before the testing begins. (If parents refuse permission, the school system may initiate legal action to compel evaluation; but this is seldom done. When parents refuse permission to have their children evaluated, the children tend to go unevaluated.)

Forms requesting parental permission for evaluation are frequently formidable. Their technical language and bureaucratic style, while conveying little information, often generate great anxiety in parents. Most parents know very little about educational assessments, psychological evaluations, and audiological, speech, and language testing. No wonder, then, when they receive "Parental Permission for Evaluation" forms like those shown on pages 35 and 36, their first reaction is often panic—quickly followed by frustration, anger, and a feeling of helplessness.

What should you do when confronted with the school's request to evaluate your child's learning needs? Maybe, you think, the school knows best. So you sign the form, grant permission to evaluate your child, and then wonder if you

```
Mr. & Mrs. Austin                    RE    Evaluation
1519 S. West Street                   SCHOOL  Westview Elementary
Alexandria, Va. 22355                 ID NO.  10094

Dear  Mr. & Mrs. Austin:
```

As we have discussed, the following individual evaluations are essential in understanding your child's particular needs.

Audiological	X
Educational	X
Psychological	X
Sociocultural	X
Speech and language	
Vision	X
Medical	X

The evaluations may include conferring with your child, testing of general ability and educational achievement, and/or an evaluation of feelings.

If you have any questions about the evaluations or why they are necessary, please call **Ms. Pilerton** at **624-5525**. When the evaluations are completed, an opportunity will be provided for you to discuss the results. You also may have access to these and any other educational records pertaining to your child.

We are not able to proceed with these evaluations until we have your permission to do so. Please return the attached form to me, at the above address, within ten working days after receipt of this letter. You do have the right to refuse to give your permission. Should you refuse to give permission, the _____ County Public Schools has the right to appeal your decision.

If a recent medical examination is required, the examination may be scheduled through a private physician—at your own expense—or through the _____ County Department of Health Services—free of charge. If you wish to schedule a free medical examination for your child, please contact **County Health** at **524-6660**.
Dept.

If you would like to be informed of the time, date, and place of subsequent meetings held to discuss your child's educational needs, contact **Ms. Pilerton** at **624-5525** who will inform you of the local screening and eligibility committee meetings.

Sincerely,

Marcia J. Pilerton
Marcia J. Pilerton
Principal
/ct

Attachment

cc: Cumulative File

did the right thing. Or maybe you refuse permission for evaluation; and again wonder if you made the right decision.

Neither of these responses is helpful to you or your child. What you need is a greater understanding of the evaluation process and a knowledge of specific actions you may take in the face of this request to evaluate your son or daughter. You need some information to consider and some steps to follow to wrestle with the issues of evaluation. Knowing what to do will reduce your feeling of helplessness and begin to let you and your child "do" something about evaluation, as opposed to being "done in" by evaluation.

PARENTAL PERMISSION FOR EVALUATION

I GIVE PERMISSION for the _____ County Public Schools to proceed with the following
evaluations for my child, _____ Sara Austin _____ :
                                    Name of Child

Audiological _____ X _____
Educational _____ X _____
Psychological _____ X _____
Sociocultural _____ X _____
Speech and language
Vision _____ X _____
Medical _____ X _____

I understand that I have the right to review my child's school records and to be informed
of the results of these evaluations. I understand that no change will be made in my
child's educational program as a result of these evaluations without my knowledge. I
understand that I have the right to refuse to give permission for these evaluations.

I have arranged to have a medical examination for my child through:
*(Please check if
a recent medical* [   ] A private physician [   ] _____ County Department of Health Services
*examination is
required)*

_____   _____
        Date   *Signature of Parent*

- -

I DO NOT GIVE PERMISSION for the _____ County Public Schools to proceed with the evaluation of my child, _____.

I understand that I have the right to review my child's school records. I understand
that the _____ County Public Schools may use established procedures to obtain authori-
zation to proceed with the evaluation and that if the _____ County Public Schools
appeals my decision, I will be notified of my due process rights.

_____   _____
        Date   *Signature of Parent*

cc: Cumulative File

THE EVALUATION PROCESS:
PURPOSES, ACTIVITIES, AND PROFESSIONALS

There may be many reasons for explaining why a child's physical, social, and
intellectual development is slow compared with that of his or her peers. Some
children merely mature more slowly than others; time will find them "catching
up." In some instances, the child's home environment and family or cultural
background may cause learning to proceed at a slower-than-average rate. Other
children may have physical impairments that interfere with their development.
Perhaps they have a visual, hearing, or orthopedic impairment. Still other chil-

dren may have retardation, learning disabilities, or severe emotional problems. Any and all of these conditions could interfere with a child's general educational and developmental progress.

The purpose of the school's evaluation process is to identify why your child is experiencing learning difficulties. While attempting to determine the source of the learning problem, additional information is developed concerning your child's present academic and developmental abilities. This information is helpful in understanding where and why your child is having problems and in planning future programs to overcome those problems.

School systems use many different tests and materials when evaluating children. In some states the tests used in evaluation may be specified by state regulations and will vary according to the child's suspected disability. Basically, however, all tests and materials may be grouped into five categories, or as schools sometimes call them, assessment components. These five categories and the professionals who gather information for each category are:

1. *The educational component:* An analysis reflecting tests and evaluation instruments that identify your child's current educational performance and specific instructional needs in academic skills, for example, reading, math, spelling, and language performance. These tests may be given by the classroom teacher, when qualified, and by educational diagnosticians trained in using these particular tests.

2. *The medical component:* An assessment from a licensed physician indicating general medical history and any medical/health problems which might impede your child's learning. Although parents usually obtain this assessment at their own expense, each school system maintains a list of physicians and clinics where free medical exams are available.

3. *The sociocultural component:* A report developed from interviews with parents, teachers, and others describing the child's background and adaptive behavior at home and in school. The report is usually prepared by a school social worker who interviews the parents at home. If parents wish, however, they may request that the interview take place elsewhere, for example, at school.

4. *The psychological component:* A report usually written by a school psychologist and based upon numerous tests and evaluation instruments assessing the child's general intelligence, ability to coordinate eye and hand movements, social skills, emotional development, and other thinking skills. When necessary, this component may also include an evaluation by a clinical psychologist or a psychiatrist.

5. *Others:* In some instances the preceding components will need to be supplemented with certain assessments in the areas of speech, language, muscle development, and the like.

Now you know, generally, the purposes, the activities, and the professionals involved in any evaluation of your child. But your interest is not a general one. Your interest is in the particular evaluation that is being proposed for your child. With this specific concern in mind, "Parent Action-Steps for Evaluation" were developed for you to follow in each of the four phases of the evaluation process: giving/refusing permission to evaluate, activities before evaluation, activities during evaluation, and activities after evaluation.

For each phase of the process, you will find a series of actions and accompanying steps you may take to participate actively and effectively in your child's evaluation. You need not, and should not, take all the actions and all the steps outlined. Look over the listing and choose those actions and steps to follow which will be most helpful to you and to your child in assuring that the evaluation is fair and thorough. Remember, these action steps are designed to allow you to "do" something constructive in the evaluation process rather than merely get "done to."

PARENT ACTION-STEPS FOR EVALUATION

Giving/Refusing Permission to Evaluate

After the school system has notified you in writing of its desire to evaluate your child, you must decide whether to give or refuse permission for this evaluation. To help you decide, you may wish:

ACTION A: To explore your feelings about evaluation, particularly this event, by

1. talking to someone close to you—your spouse, a friend, another parent;
2. talking to a helping professional—a teacher, counselor, minister, advocate;
3. reading through your child's previous evaluation records.

ACTION B: To learn more about your local evaluation process by

1. identifying the school-system person most responsible for your child's evaluation;
2. obtaining all relevant written policies and procedures from the person in Step 1, the school's public information officer, or the department of special education;
3. obtaining parent handbooks and pamphlets on evaluation;
4. making a list of all your questions;
5. meeting with a knowledgeable person—an experienced parent, a school representative, an advocate—to discuss evaluation;
6. diagramming your understanding of the steps and sequence of your school's evaluation procedures.

ACTION C: To learn more about the evaluation planned for your child by

1. requiring in writing from school officials the reasons for this evaluation;
2. requiring a detailed plan for evaluation, to include:
   a. areas to be evaluated;
   b. tests or portions of tests to be used;
   c. reasons for selecting tests;
   d. qualifications of persons giving tests;
   e. statement as to how evaluation will be structured to compensate for your child's suspected disability.

ACTION D: To assess the appropriateness of the evaluation tests by

1. consulting a knowledgeable parent or independent professional;
2. reviewing literature on evaluation;
3. previewing the test with a school psychologist.

ACTION E: To explore the independent evaluation alternative by

1. considering your feelings about independent evaluations, especially the cost;
2. learning about your right to an independent evaluation;
3. learning your school's procedures for providing independent evaluations;
4. talking with parents whose children have had independent evaluations;
5. consulting an evaluator in private practice.

This list of action-steps is merely suggestive of activities other parents have found helpful when deciding whether to give or withhold permission for having their children evaluated by the school system. You should undertake only those actions and steps that: (1) make sense to you; (2) will help you make a confident decision; and (3) will give you a feeling of managing, rather than being managed by, the evaluation process. Not all actions and steps should be initiated at one time; doing too much may indicate your desire to avoid making a decision.

Before Evaluation

Once you have given permission for your child to be evaluated by the school system or have arranged for an independent evaluation, you can do several things before the evaluation to help make the experience a comfortable and productive one for your child and you. You may wish:

ACTION A: To anticipate your child's needs in this evaluation by

1. making lists of what was difficult and what was manageable or helpful in previous evaluations;
2. talking with your spouse, your child's therapist or teacher, or an earlier evaluator about how he handles evaluations, specifically his:
   a. reaction to strangers
   b. tolerance for testing demands
   c. ability to sit still for long periods
   d. response to doctors and other professionals
   e. fatigue threshold—how long until he gets too tired to work at his best
   f. need for an interpreter if non–English-speaking or a user of sign language
   g. ability to separate from you, to leave and stay with a stranger
   h. high and low points in the day;
3. reading pamphlets or articles on children and evaluation;
4. talking with your child about prior evaluation experiences;
5. talking with your child about his thoughts about the new evaluation.

ACTION B: To prepare yourself for this evaluation by

1. talking to other parents about their experiences;
2. seeking tips on rough spots and how to work around them from an organization for parents of handicapped children;
3. discussing your concerns with a friend;

4. discussing the responsibilities with your spouse and dividing up the work-load;
5. listing your practical concerns, such as:
   a. schedules
   b. costs
   c. child care
   d. transportation
   e. obtaining an interpreter
   f. appropriate dress
   g. food during the evaluation;
6. learning the evaluation facility's expectation for your participation;
7. considering various roles you might choose or need to assume, such as
   a. observer of your child
   b. active participant in testing
   c. supporter and comforter to your child
   d. information source about your child;
8. asking a friend to accompany you to the evaluation.

ACTION C: To plan for your child's individualized evaluation with a representative of the evaluation facility by

1. arranging for a meeting or a phone conference;
2. preparing for this meeting by listing your questions and concerns in priority order;
3. asking a friend or advocate to accompany you;
4. requesting information on or clarification of the evaluation process;
5. sharing your plans for your participation;
6. raising concerns you might have over keeping the experience a positive one for your child;
7. insisting that your high-priority concerns be addressed;
8. making final plans for the evaluation.

ACTION D: To prepare your child for the evaluation by

1. talking together about the reasons for and process of this new evaluation;
2. providing opportunities for your child to express feelings and ask questions;
3. making a preevaluation visit together to explore the evaluation facility and meet testers;
4. giving your child the chance to make choices about
   a. what to wear
   b. what to take for a snack
   c. what toy or book to take;
5. planning a postevalution event together.

Again, you are cautioned not to try all actions and all steps. Selective use of these activities will focus your efforts and save your energy for the most important matters.

During Evaluation

You and your child have arrived at the facility where the evaluation will take place. Here the actions and steps you select will be strongly influenced by the age of your child and his past experience with evaluations. Keeping in mind your child's age and personality you may wish:

ACTION A: To ease your child into the situation by

1. allowing him to become familiar with the areas he will be in—waiting room, playroom, testing room, examination room, rest room;
2. introducing him to one or two of the adults with whom he will be working;
3. reviewing the day's plan with him;
4. reassuring him that you will be available to him at all times;
5. encouraging him to ask questions and share worries.

ACTION B: To monitor the evaluation process by

1. requesting that the evaluation start on time;
2. requiring that the schedule of activities be followed;
3. inquiring as to any changes in personnel or instruments to be used;
4. observing testing of your child whenever possible;
5. recording your impressions of your child's performance;
6. recording your impressions of each evaluator's handling of your child.

ACTION C: To protect your child by

1. keeping an eye on his fatigue and stress levels;
2. staying with him during medical procedures—shots, blood tests, EEG;
3. requiring explanations of mysterious, scary, or unexpected procedures;
4. letting him come to you;
5. taking breaks for rest, refreshment, and going to the bathroom;
6. demanding that highly negative experiences be cut short;
7. deciding when your child has had enough for the day.

After Evaluation

When the evaluation is completed parents and children usually have a need to feel that the ordeal is truly completed and has been worthwhile. There are numerous ways you and your family can wrap up the evaluation experience and begin to use the information gained from the evaluation for educational planning. You may wish:

ACTION A: To help your child round out the experience on a positive note by

1. encouraging him to review the experience through storytelling, pictures, or dramatic play;
2. discussing with him the people and activities he liked and disliked;
3. sharing your own feelings and perceptions of the experience;
4. making a list of his successes;
5. informing him of the evaluation results—what was learned about his strengths and needs;
6. throwing an end-of-evaluation party.

ACTION B: To help yourself complete the experience by

1. recounting the experience to a friend or parent support group;
2. checking the actual evaluation experience against what you had planned or anticipated;
3. writing a letter to the evaluation facility describing your sense of the strengths and needs of the process;
4. giving yourself a graduation-from-evaluation gift.

ACTION C: To prepare for your parent conference with the evaluation team by

1. reviewing prior evaluation findings on your child;
2. reviewing your information and notes on this evaluation;
3. anticipating areas of stronger and weaker performance by your child in this evaluation;

4. obtaining the record of this evaluation, including individual reports;
5. reading the record to see that it is
    a. accurate
    b. complete
    c. bias free
    d. jargon free
    e. current
    f. consistent
    g. understandable
    h. non-judgmental;
6. noting your concerns in the form of questions to be asked at the parent conference;
7. choosing a friend to go with you to the parent conference.

To help you systematically negotiate the evaluation phase of the special education maze, a Parent Action-Steps for Evaluation Chart follows. The chart has space for writing each action and step you will take in the evaluation phase. At the end of the chart is a section for names, phone numbers, and dates related to those actions and steps. The chart allows you to plan steps you choose to take in your child's evaluation, to monitor the progress of the evaluation, and to maintain a record of how and when the evaluation was conducted and completed—all useful information.

**PARENT ACTION STEPS
FOR EVALUATION CHART
(WORKSHEET)**

Phase I: Giving/Refusing Permission to Evaluate

Action: _____
_____

Step: _____
Step: _____
Action: _____
_____

Step: _____
Step: _____
Action: _____
_____

Step: _____
Step: _____

Phase II: Before Evaluation

Action: _____

_____

Step: _____

Step: _____

Action: _____

_____

Step: _____

Step: _____

Action: _____

_____

Step: _____

Step: _____

Phase III: During Evaluation

Action: _____

_____

Step: _____

Step: _____

Action: _____

_____

Step: _____

Step: _____

Action: _____

_____

Step: _____

Step: _____

Phase IV: After Evaluation

Action: _____

_____

Step: _____

Step: _____

Action: _____

_____

Step: _____

Step: _____

Action: _____

_____

Step: _____

Step: _____

Important Telephone Numbers: *Important Dates:*

_____   _____
_____   _____
_____   _____
_____   _____
_____   _____

FORMAL
EVALUATION REQUIREMENTS

As you undertake the action-steps for evaluation, you should understand that all school systems must follow certain procedures when evaluating a child. If school officials fail to meet any of these requirements, you can take various actions, described in Chapter 7, to require them to fulfill their evaluation duties.

First among the required duties in evaluation, the administrator of special education must inform you in your native language and by your primary means of communication—vocal, sign language, or Braille—of:

1. the school's desire to evaluate your child;
2. your rights as parents pertaining to special education for your child; and
3. the need for your consent prior to evaluation.

Second, the school system must insure its evaluation procedures provide:

1. your written consent prior to evaluation;
2. the assignment of surrogate parents (after a formal hearing), when you refuse or are not available for protecting the interests of your child;
3. confidentiality of all evaluation results;
4. an opportunity for you to obtain an independent evaluation of your child if you believe the school's evaluation to be biased or invalid;
5. an opportunity for you to have a hearing to question evaluation results with which you disagree;
6. an opportunity for you to examine your child's official school records; and
7. testing that does not discriminate against your child because of racial or cultural bias or because the tests are inappropriate for a person with your child's disabilities.

Third, the school system must have policies and procedures to guarantee that the tests and other evaluation materials used with your child:

1. are provided and administered in your child's native language and primary means of communication, unless clearly unfeasible;
2. have been professionally approved for the specific purposes for which they are used; and

3. are administered by trained professionals in conformance with the instructions of the persons who produced the tests and material.

Finally, the evaluation procedure should meet the following conditions:

1. Tests and evaluation materials should be used that assess a wide range of educational and developmental needs and capabilities in addition to tests designed to provide a single general intelligence quotient.
2. Tests should be selected and administered so as to insure that when they are administered they accurately reflect the child's aptitude, achievement level, or whatever other factors they are designed to measure, rather than reflecting the child's handicapping conditions.
3. The evaluation should be undertaken by a team or group of persons from several professional backgrounds, including at least one teacher or other specialist with knowledge in the area of your child's suspected disability. Your child should be assessed in all areas related to the suspected disability, including, where appropriate, health, vision, hearing, social, and emotional status, general intelligence, academic performance, communication skills, and motor abilities.

These are the minimal requirements school officials must meet when evaluating your child to receive special education services. The regulations of your state or local school district may include additional procedures. Therefore, before initiating your action-steps for evaluation, review the rules and regulations carefully.

THE EVALUATION CONFERENCE

Once the formal evaluation of your child has been completed, many school jurisdictions will call a meeting or conference with you to explain the results of the testing. If no such meeting is suggested by your school system, you should request one. Unless you fully understand the results and conclusions drawn from the evaluation, you will have no idea whether your child needs or is eligible for special education services.

Your effective participation in all the remaining phases of the special education process depends in large part on how well you understand your child's learning problems. Before you can confidently work with school officials during the eligibility, IEP, and placement meetings, you need to know your child's current abilities and problems—as they are known by school personnel. Therefore, before proceeding to any other meetings after the evaluation of your child is completed, make certain someone has explained to your complete satisfaction the results and conclusions of the evaluation process.

THE NEXT STEP

To this point, you have collected information about your child derived from two primary sources: personal observations of your child made by you and other persons and observations arising from the formal evaluation process. Even when the results of the evaluation have been interpreted for you, you still may worry about remembering all that was said. Luckily, the school system does not depend solely upon the memory of its professional staff to recall specific children, their progress, and their needs. The memory of the school system is contained within its official records.

Schools are required by law to maintain certain records. They are also required by law, called the Family Educational Rights and Privacy Act or the Buckley Amendment, to make these records available to you upon request. School records offer significant information to parents about their children. School systems often place great weight upon information in these records when making educational decisions. For these reasons parents must know how to obtain, interpret, and correct these records and how to use them effectively in eligibility determination meetings. In Chapter 4 you will find guidance for the corridor in the maze of special education pertaining to school records.

School Records
and Reports

Journals
of the Journey

OBTAINING YOUR CHILD'S RECORDS
FROM THE LOCAL SCHOOL*

Every school jurisdiction has a written policy associated with the management and confidentiality of records. Included in the policy is a procedure for parents to use to gain access to confidential records. Getting copies of your child's school records should be virtually automatic. You first need to inquire about the location of your child's confidential file or record. This is best done by asking the principal in your child's school. The principal will have the local school's *cumulative* file, which you will want to see and/or copy. Often the cumulative file contains little more than a profile card with personal identification data and perhaps academic achievement levels, some teacher reports and report cards, and a copy of your child's Individualized Education Program (IEP), if he or she is already in special education.

*Material in this section has been drawn extensively from the booklet *Your School Records* (Washington, D.C.: Children's Defense Fund, 1978).

The *confidential* file may also be kept at your child's school, or in a central administrative office where the special education program offices are located. The information about the location of records should be readily available from your school principal or superintendent's office. The confidential record contains all of the reports written as a result of the school's evaluation; reports of independent evaluators, if this applies; medical records that you have had released; summary reports of eligibility/evaluation team meetings; and, often, correspondence between you and school officials.

Some school systems keep the reports of eligibility meetings, correspondence between the parents and school officials, and other similar documents in a separate *compliance* file. A good bit of detective work is sometimes required to understand your school system's individual filing system!

Once you know the location of the records, how do you best proceed to obtain copies of the confidential file? If you want to get a copy of your child's records through the mail, you will most likely be required to sign a release-of-information form. This can be obtained by calling or writing the appropriate office. Other school systems will send records upon receiving a written statement from parents requesting release of information. For this service, a school system can charge you only for the cost of reproducing and mailing the records, not for personnel time or other indirect costs to the school system.

Another way to obtain a copy of your child's confidential record is by appointment. A telephone call to the appropriate office requesting a mutually convenient time for you to review and to copy the record often results in a professional person being on hand to guide you through the records and to answer any questions. Again, the only cost to you will be the reproduction costs.

Parents sometimes ask, "Wouldn't it be better if I go into the office unannounced to see the record?" Several issues arise in this situation.

1. Parents are concerned that parts of the record will be removed if prior notice is given to the school system and replaced following the appointment. Isolated cases such as this have indeed been reported. However, the good faith of both parents and school systems are needed in this area. Should problems develop, mechanisms exist whereby records of questionable value to the child can be challenged and removed with the consent of both parties.

2. School systems are required to make records available within forty-five days. Most systems respond to a parent's request within two to five days. Schools are not required to show you your child's records on demand, but often they will accommodate you in the case of an emergency.

3. A school office, like any office, is run most efficiently when the needs of the people working there are taken into consideration. A parent, arriving unannounced, asking for services that involve the time of office or professional personnel, can interrupt important routines and schedules. By asking for an appointment parents continue to build the bridge of mutual respect and consideration needed in effective educational advocacy.

Once you have gained access to your child's records, does this mean you can see any and all records pertaining to your child? Just what records is the school system legally required to show you?

Under the Buckley Amendment, schools must show parents all records, files, documents, and other materials that are maintained by the school system and contain information relating to their children. This includes all records referring to your child in any personally identifiable manner, that is, records containing your child's name, social security number, student ID, or other data making them traceable to your child. Excluded from the records schools must show you, however, are the following: (1) notes of teachers, counselors, and/or school administrators made for their personal use and *shown* to nobody else; (2) records of school security police when they are kept separate from other school records, and used only for law-enforcement purposes within the local area, and when security police have no access to any other school files; and (3) personnel records of school employees.

Items one and three of these exclusions often cause parents much trouble. Frequently, parents whose children are evaluated by school psychologists want to see the test papers their children wrote. Psychologists often refuse to show parents these papers, saying the tests fall within the personal-notes exemption or that the tests are copyrighted and cannot be disclosed to nonprofessionals. According to the Office of the General Counsel, U.S. Department of Education, test papers (protocols) completed in psychological evaluations and maintained in personally identifiable form are educational records under the Buckley Amendment. Therefore, upon your request psychologists must show you the test papers and other materials completed by your child during his evaluation.

Similarly, parents often feel they should be able to examine the personal records of their child's teacher to assess the teacher's academic qualifications and experience. But these records are exempt from such review under the Buckley Amendment and are not open to parental examination. (*Note:* If either the "raw scores" from evaluations of your child or the qualifications of your child's teachers become issues in due process hearings, parents may obtain these data either from the files or from direct examination of witnesses during the hearing. More about this in Chapter 6.)

EXAMINING AND CORRECTING
YOUR CHILD'S RECORDS

Even when you have your child's records in your hands, you may wonder what you've got. The language of the educators, psychologists, educational diagnosticians, and other school professionals often appears unintelligible at best and nonsense at worst. If this is the case for you, all you need do is ask someone to help you. The law requires school officials to explain the records to you when you do not understand them. Or you may take a friend or a professional person with you to help review the records and explain unintelligible parts. When you do this, however, you will be asked to sign a form giving that person permission to see your child's records.

As you review the records, certain material may appear inaccurate, biased, incomplete, inconsistent, or just plain wrong. If this happens, you can follow two paths to address the problem. First, you can ask the school officials informally to delete the material, giving your reasons for the request. Often school officials will honor the request and no problem arises. If difficulties do develop and school officials refuse to remove the requested material, your second approach to correcting the records is the formal hearing.

When you ask for a formal hearing, you should do so in writing, with a letter addressed to the school principal or the school official designated in your school's written procedures. Be certain to keep a copy of the letter for your files. The hearing you request will involve a meeting between you and school officials, presided over by a hearing officer. The hearing officer in this case may include any person, even an official of the school system, who does not have a direct interest in the outcome of the hearing. The purpose of the hearing is to allow you and the school system to present evidence about the school record in dispute and to let the hearing officer determine who is right.

Under the Buckley Amendment, the school must schedule a hearing on any disputed records within a "reasonable" time, and you must be notified of the time and place of the hearing "reasonably" in advance. What is "reasonable" in your school system will be spelled out in your local school or state board of education regulations. These same regulations will also explain: (1) your right to have someone, even an attorney, assist or represent you at the hearing; (2) the length of time the school system has to make its decision after the hearing; and (3) the requirement that the hearing officer must include in the decision a discussion of the evidence and reasons for deciding the matter as he did.

Since the hearing officer at a records hearing may be a school official, parents often feel that the proceedings smack of a "kangaroo court." Although unfair decisions have been rendered, more often than not the hearing officer will act impartially in deciding the issue. Even if parents lose their request to have a record removed, further actions may be taken to reduce the negative impact of the report felt to be defective.

The most effective way to handle this problem is "to insert into the record a written statement concerning your objections to the material, indicating why you think it is false, misleading or inappropriate. The school is required by law to keep your statement with the record and release it to everyone who gets the contested record."*   In this manner you can be assured that anyone seeing the record will be informed of your objection to its contents.

Your School Records (Washington, D.C.: Children's Defense Fund, 1978), p. 7.

Besides amending the disputed record, you can take two other steps when you believe your "reasonable" requests to correct the records have been improperly refused. You can send a letter of complaint to:

Family Educational Rights and Privacy Act Office (FERPA)
Department of Health and Human Services
300 Independence Ave., S.W.
Washington, DC 20201

This office is responsible for enforcing the Buckley Amendment and will look into your complaint. A second action you can take in some areas is to sue in court. This option differs in various parts of the country, so you should consult an attorney to see if such action is possible where you live. In both these last options, however, significant time is required before action occurs. Therefore, if you use them, you should also amend the record in anticipation of having it removed later.

CONTROLLING
WHO SEES YOUR CHILD'S RECORDS

The Buckley Amendment prohibits schools from disclosing your child's records to anyone without your written consent. The only exceptions are:

1. school officials (including teachers) in the same district with a "legitimate educational interest," as defined in the school procedures;
2. school officials in the school district to which your child intends to transfer (but only *after* you have had a chance to request a copy of the records and to challenge their contents);
3. certain state and national *education* agencies, if necessary for enforcing federal laws;
4. anyone to whom a state statute requires the school to report information;
5. accrediting and research organizations helping the school, provided they guarantee confidentiality;
6. student financial aid officials;
7. those with court orders, provided the school makes "reasonable" efforts to notify the parent or student before releasing the records;
8. appropriate people in health and safety emergencies.

According to federal law, police, probation officers, and employers cannot see or receive information from your child's records without your consent. The exception to this rule is where your state has a law, passed before November 19, 1974, *requiring* (not just permitting) schools to give them such data. If such a law exists in your state, your school can provide this information without your consent.

With that exception, schools must have your permission to release material from your child's records to persons other than yourself. When requesting the release of those records, the school must tell you the records involved, why they have been requested, and who will receive them. Likewise, if you want someone outside the school system to see your child's records, you will be asked to sign a release granting such permission. All these precautions have been instituted to protect your privacy and that of your child.

WHEN YOU MOVE

As a parent of a handicapped child, you have a special interest in knowing what material is contained in your child's school records. This is true because of the emphasis placed on these records when deciding a child's eligibility for special education services. Thus, you should annually review your child's records to make sure they are up to date, accurate, and so forth. You should also be certain you have a duplicate copy of all the material in the official files. In this way if the records are lost, as they easily can be in a large school system, you will have copies to replace them.

In today's society people are always on the move. Your child's school records, of course, will move with you. To be certain your child's new school receives only relevant and current records, you should examine the records and identify specifically the material you want forwarded. Most school systems will honor your request and send only the information you want released. Should they wish to send material you want withheld, you can initiate the hearing procedure described earlier to prohibit their action. In any case, before you move, *always* review your child's school folder and eliminate the irrelevant, inaccurate, and dated material or attach your critique to those records you believe should be removed.

A FINAL NOTE: THICK RECORDS

Classroom teachers have been heard to comment, "When I see a thick set of records of a child new to my class, I know trouble is coming." This is another reason for your diligence in annually reviewing your child's records. Many reports, especially those written several years previously, give little if any information that will be useful in current decisions about your child. A careful weeding out of irrelevant documents can help to avoid the "thick record syndrome."

THE FOUR-STEP RECORD DECODER

When you have obtained the school's records, often a stack of documents an inch or more thick, what in heaven's name will you do with them? How can you begin to make sense of all this material written about your child? You have organized your home observations of your child into a framework; now you will organize the school's observations of your child by employing the Four-Step Record Decoder. The decoder helps you organize, read, analyze, and evaluate your child's school records.

Organize

1. After obtaining the complete set of records from the school system, separate the reports describing your child (teacher reports, psychological evaluations, social history, etc.) from other documents or correspondence.
2. Make an extra copy of the records. In this way you will have an original and a copy you can mark, cut, paste, and use however it will help you.
3. Arrange each set, reports and extra documents, in chronological order.
4. Secure the pages in a folder with a clip or in a looseleaf notebook so that if you drop them—heaven forbid—you won't have to back up three steps.
5. Number each report and make a chronological list that can be added onto as new records are generated. The list might look like this:

Educational Reports of Susan Martin

REPORT	DATE	REPORTING PERSON
1. Psychoeducational evaluation	5/3/82	Katherine Conner
2. Teacher's report	5/82	Cathy Porterman
3. Sociological report	5/12/82	Patricia Roberts
4. Psychiatric evaluation summary	6/08/82	Dr. Gerald Brown
5. Pupil contact report	6/14/82	Katherine Conner
6. Psychological evaluation summary	8/23/82	Dr. Ronald McPherson
7. Teacher's report	9/14/82	Dru Dunn
8. Psychologist's memorandum	9/14/82	Barbara Hager

Read

1. Read through the entire record to get overall impressions and tones of the school's view of your child.
2. In the margins of your working copy, mark with a question mark the statements or areas of the reports you do not understand or with which you disagree.

Analyze

1. While rereading the reports, underline the phrases or sentences you feel best describe *both* your child's strengths and your child's problems. Put an S in the margin opposite a description of your child's learning strengths, a P opposite the problems. When you come to a phrase or sentence reporting your child's learning style, write LS in the margin.

2. Using a worksheet similar to the one on pages 58 and 59, place these phrases or sentences about your child's strengths and problems within the developmental categories of movement, communications, social relationships, self-concept/independence, perception/senses, thinking skills, and learning style.

3. After each piece of data put the *source* and *date*. Often you will find trends beginning to emerge. The same observation, said in similar language, may occur in several reports over a period of time. You can indicate this by simply recording additional sources and dates to the original data.

4. List *recommendations* made by each evaluator in the last section of the analysis sheet. Recommendations might include services needed, classroom environment, class size, type of school setting, recommendation for further testing, specific teaching materials or equipment.

Evaluate

Using the question-mark notations you have made in the margins and your overall sense of the records from your analytical work with them, evaluate their accuracy against the following criteria:

ACCURATE   Do the reports and portions of the records correspond with your own feelings, perceptions, observations, and assessments of your child?

COMPLETE   Are all the documents required by the school system for the eligibility, Individualized Education Program, and placement decision available in the file? For example, medical report, social history, psychological examination, educational report, and others as required.

BIAS FREE   Are the reports free from cultural or racial bias? Do they reflect a consideration of the effect your child's disability might have had upon the outcome or results of the tests?

JARGON FREE   Do the reports describe your child in nontechnical terms and/or language you can understand and use? (Examples of jargon and technical terms are: splayed fingers, dyslexia, gestalt, perceptual-motor dysfunction, figure ground, and the like.) In a good report technical language used will be defined within the report.

NONJUDGMENTAL   Does the report reflect a respect for your child and your family? Does it avoid the use of language that judges rather than describes? (Examples of judgmental statements: She is fickle. He is incorrigible. The mother is unstable.)

FOUR-STEP RECORD DECODER

Data	Source	Date
MOVEMENT Strengths Problems		
COMMUNICATIONS Strengths Problems		
SOCIAL RELATIONSHIPS Strengths Problems		
SELF-CONCEPT/INDEPENDENCE Strengths Problems		

FOUR-STEP RECORD DECODER

Data	Source	Date
SENSES/PERCEPTION Strengths Problems		
THINKING SKILLS Strengths Problems		
LEARNING STYLE Strengths Problems		
RECOMMENDATIONS:		

FOUR-STEP RECORD DECODER

Data		Source	Date
MOVEMENT Strengths	1) She can catch a bounced ball 2) She can kick a stationary ball 3) Walks forward on a four foot walking board	1-3) Mr. Terrence Adaptive P.E. Specialist	1/81
Problems	1) fine motor - trouble drawing and integrating complicated figures 2) gross motor - long for her age - gives appearance of being uncoordinated 3) difficulty in integrating motor skills to form motor plan act 4) difficulty jumping rope	1-2) Ms. Lothian - psychological test 3) Mr. Terrence - P.E. 4) Mrs. Mulroney - P.E. Teacher report	1/81 2/80 11/81
COMMUNICATIONS Strengths	1) Sara has significant improvement in syntax 2) She eagerly participated in class using age appropriate vocabulary	1) Mrs. Find - speech therapist 2) Mr. Chase - Sp. Ed. teacher report	6/81 6/81
Problems	1) the problem may be in processing or word finding 2) there is a lag in expressive language - difficulty expressing ideas maybe language retrieval problems 3) Poor word finding skills, poor sequencing skills poor auditory memory and association abilities	1) County Health Dept. report 2) Ms. Lacey - Sp.ed teacher report 3) Mrs. Find - speech therapist	8/79 5/80 1/81
SOCIAL RELATIONSHIPS Strengths	1) She seems happy, is generally accepted by classmates - has maintained friendships in school 2) Sara is people oriented, although on an observing type basis	1) Ms. Chase - Sp.Ed. teacher report 2) Ms. Lothian - psychological test	6/81 1/81
Problems	1) She frequently tells peers what to do, and makes negative comments about herself when she makes mistakes	1) Mrs. Lacey - Sp.Ed. teacher report	5/80
SELF-CONCEPT/INDEPENDENCE Strengths	1) She works well in a small, structured, positive environment and needs to continue to build a positive self-image	1) Ms. Chase - Sp.Ed. teacher's report	6/81
Problems	1) Sara's present difficulty is that she feels different, abnormal and rejected 2) Extreme need for nurturance and to feel good about herself	1-2) Ms. Lothian - psychological test	1/81

Data	Source	Date
SENSES/PERCEPTION **Strengths** 1) On Bender-Gestalt test she could copy figures and make them recognizable, despite difficulties she experienced with integration and distortions	1) Dr. Hackett, private psychologist	11/80
Problems 1) She doesn't remember details from pictures she sees or stories she has read 2) On Bender-Gestalt - Hackett her planning is haphazard and unorganized, her production inconsistent	1) Mrs. Chase, Sp. Ed. teacher's report 2) Mr. Lothian, psychological test	1/81 1/81
THINKING SKILLS **Strengths** 1) In reading her decoding skills are excellent. She has good sight vocabulary 2) She has learned addition and subtraction facts - is now learning 2's, 3's, 5's and 10's in multiplication	1) Mrs. Chase, Sp Ed. teacher report 2)	6/81
Problems 1) She has difficulty following multiple oral directions 2) Her poor memory has caused some problems with remembering math processed 3) She has difficulty ordering ideas and retrieving some words	1) Mrs. Chase Sp. Ed. teacher report 2) 3) "	6/81
LEARNING STYLE 1) She needs a small, structured environment 2) She is eager to complete work but often perseverates on favorite assignments 3) Her planning is haphazard and unorganized	1) Mrs. Chase, Sp. Ed. teacher report 2) 3) Mr. Lothian, psychological test	6/81 1/81
RECOMMENDATIONS: 1) Helping her break down oral and written directions, repeating them to her, and having her repeat them are helpful techniques 2) In reading use sight approach, context clues, language experience stories	1) Mrs. Lothian, psychological test 2) Mrs. Lacey, Sp Ed. teacher	1/81 1/81

CURRENT   Are the dates on the records recent enough to give a report of your child's present behavior and functioning?

CONSISTENT   Is there consistency between the descriptions of your child given by each evaluator? Or do you find contradictions and differences of opinion?

UNDERSTANDABLE   Is the language used meaningful, clear, and understandable to you? (Example of an unclear statement: "She appears to have a psychological learning disability, calling for treatment involving a moderation of the special focus on interpersonal sensitivity she has received so far." *What does that mean?*)

OVERALL INTEGRITY   Considering the record as a whole, does it make sense and lead to the given recommendations?

An example of the analysis sheets of the Record Decoder Sara's parents worked out are found on pages 60 and 61.

By completing your own Record Decoder analysis sheets, you will become thoroughly familiar with your child as seen through the "close-up lens" of his school records. The information contained in those records provides the basis upon which crucial decisions will be made concerning your child's education. The importance of organizing, reading, analyzing, and evaluating your child's school records cannot be overemphasized. Before you continue to the next phase of the maze, make sure the information in your child's file paints an accurate picture of him.

EVALUATION TROUBLESHOOTING

After you have reviewed your child's latest evaluation reports and examined past evaluations in the school file using the Four-Step Record Decoder, you will conclude one of two things. Either you agree that the evaluation results are accurate, complete, consistent, and up to date; or you believe they are deficient in some respect. If you believe the evaluation materials are satisfactory, you move to the next corridor of the special education maze—eligibility determination. But what if you think the evaluation findings are inadequate? What steps do you take next?

You can select one of two paths in attempting to correct the defects you find with the evaluations. One path is informal—you informally ask school officials to remove the faulty evaluation from the record, or undertake additional evaluations, or add materials you provide to the file, or possibly just clarify for you the deficiencies you see existing in the evaluation findings. Should this approach fail, you can seek to resolve your difficulties through a more formal approach.

EVALUATION

agree — **disagree**

On to eligibility

formal — **Informal**

formal	Informal
1. Ask for record removal	1. Hearing to remove
2. Ask for added evaluation	2. Request independent evaluation at public expense
3. Ask that material be added	
4. Ask for clarification	3. Secure independent evaluation at personal expense

Where your problem involves earlier evaluations now a part of your child's official school file, you can seek to amend the records by employing the formal process for correcting records described earlier. Where your concern is the inadequacy of the school's most recent evaluation, however, you can request that an independent evaluation of your child be made at public expense.

Federal and state law both provide parents the opportunity to obtain an independent evaluation of their child when they believe the school's evaluation is inadequate. An independent evaluation is one made by professionals *not employed by the school system.* State and local school regulations usually identify specifically the professionals or organizations whose personnel may be selected by parents to conduct the independent evaluation. Often these evaluations will be undertaken by the county or state departments of health or mental health. The steps you should follow to secure the independent evaluation are outlined in your state regulations. *But remember!* An independent evaluation paid for at public expense *does not* mean that you, the parent, can choose whomever you wish to make an evaluation of your child. Don't run out and have an evaluation made and send the bill to your school system. If you want an independent evaluation, begin by requesting one from school officials.

Will school officials agree to an independent evaluation? Not always. On the other hand, before school officials can deny your request, they must hold a due process hearing and prove to the hearing officer the appropriateness of their evaluations. Unless the school system convenes such a hearing and proves the appropriateness of its evaluation, it cannot deny your request for an independent evaluation. *Remember!* You don't have to prove that the school's evaluation results are incorrect before asking for an independent evaluation—you are entitled to an independent evaluation if you merely believe the school system's findings are inadequate. If school officials don't wish to agree to the independent evaluation, *they must initiate the hearing procedure to justify denying the request.*

63

If you can obtain an independent evaluation at public expense, why would you ever want to pay for one out of your own pocket? Several reasons could lead a parent to seek an evaluation paid for at personal expense. First, you can personally choose the professionals who will make the evaluation. This often gives you greater confidence in the findings and allows you to select the specialist most appropriate for working with your child. Second, when you pay for your own evaluation, you can control who sees the results of the evaluation. When an independent evaluation is made at public expense, the findings must be considered by the school system in making educational decisions regarding your child. Further, the independent, publicly financed evaluation may be presented as evidence in a due process hearing. If you feel that the independent evaluation is also incorrect, you have no way to stop its being used by the school system or the hearing officer. In contrast, if you undertake your own personally financed evaluation of your child, *you* determine how those results are used and who gets to see them. Thus, if you conclude that the results accurately describe your child, you may submit the results for consideration by the school system or a hearing officer. If you are not confident of the findings, you do not have to submit them to the school or the hearing officer, unless required to do so by the hearing officer.

Although numerous benefits occur when you pay for your child's evaluation, you must weigh these benefits against several potential costs before deciding to have your own evaluation. One major cost is the dollar outlay itself. Complete educational evaluations may cost $300 or more. When the evaluation merely confirms the school's findings, it may, in fact, be beneficial—it gives more reason to believe the initial testing results—but it is an expensive procedure for securing such confirmation. Still another cost occurs when you introduce findings from your own specialists, and these findings are given little or no significance by school-system officials or the hearing officer. The excuse sometimes given for downplaying the importance of such evaluation data is reflected in the comments made by one school official in a due process hearing. According to that official, "Parents can shop around until they find a psychologist or other professional who will say exactly what they want to hear." If the school official or hearing officer with whom you are working has this attitude, the benefits of the evaluation you pay for may not equal their costs.

One last word about obtaining your own evaluations. Never have the evaluation results sent to school officials before you have examined them. On more than one occasion parents have done this to save time, only to discover that the evaluation results worked to their child's disadvantage. Therefore, discuss the evaluation findings with the professionals who developed them. Then, and only then, decide whether you want the results sent to the school system or the hearing officer.

Chapter 5

Passport to the Maze

The Eligibility Decision

INTRODUCTION

In the educational planning cycle, you have passed through the first two phases—referral and evaluation. You have gathered data at home and examined the school records and other evaluations with the Four-Step Record Decoder. Now comes phase three—*eligibility*.

The eligibility decision is usually made by a committee. The committee is known by different names in different states; for example, Eligibility Committee, M Team, Placement Committee, ARD Committee. The exact name for this committee and its composition and procedures will be found in your local or state regulations.

The procedure followed by the committee to determine your child's eligibility for special education is simple to describe in theory, and often impossible to describe in practice. In theory, here is how the committee operates. Most states include in their state regulations for special education a series of "definitions of handicapping conditions." For example, the Commonwealth of Virginia includes in its regulations definitions for the following handicapping conditions: deaf, deaf-blind, hard of hearing, mentally retarded, multi-handicapped, orthopedically impaired, other health impaired, seriously emotionally disturbed, specific learning disability, speech impaired, and visually handicapped.

Each of these conditions is then defined in the regulations. "Mentally retarded means significantly subaverage general intellectual functioning existing concurrently with deficits in adaptive behavior and manifested during the developmental period, which adversely affects a child's educational performance." If you don't understand this definition or any of the others, which may be equally obscure, ask the school officials to translate them for you. A translation of the preceding definition of "mentally retarded" might read as follows: "An IQ remaining below a score 68 to 70 for several years. In addition to the low IQ score, the child also shows problems in language and social and other behaviors, all of which have adversely affected the ability to learn."

Remember, when you don't understand the definition of the handicapping condition your child is believed to have, ask to have the definition clarified. You may be surprised to learn that school personnel are often themselves uncertain as to what the definition means. If such is the case, it is important information to uncover.

Each member of the eligibility committee receives copies of the evaluation reports and other relevant information contained in your child's official school file. The evaluation reports usually suggest the existence of one or more handicapping conditions or they imply the absence of conditions severe enough to warrant special education services. The job of the eligibility committee is to compare the results and conclusions of the evaluation against the definitions of handicapping conditions. If the results correspond with the definitions, your child will be eligible for special education services. Should the committee conclude that the results of the evaluation do not meet the definitional criteria, your child will be found ineligible for special education.

ELIGIBILITY IN ACTION: A CASE STUDY

Billy Bob Boswell is nine years old. His parents first noticed he was slow in development when he was two. Billy Bob always has taken longer and expended much more effort to learn things his brothers and sisters seem to pick up with ease. He has speech problems and still is unable to use complete sentences. From the time he entered school, he received private speech lessons. Because of continuing problems in school his teacher suggested he be evaluated for special services. Mr. and Mrs. Boswell agreed with the recommendation and signed permission for the evaluation to take place.

Tests of general intelligence showed Billy Bob to have an IQ of 105. Other tests showed him to have perceptual difficulties in coordinating his eyes and hands when copying geometric figures; problems coordinating his hands to catch a ball and his feet to stand on one leg; and difficulty in remembering things he had heard or read. Academic achievement tests found Billy Bob to be two years behind his peers in reading and arithmetic.

In Billy Bob's home state of Virginia, regulations define a "specific learning disability" as:

> a disorder in one or more of the basic psychological processes involved in understanding or in using language, spoken or written, which may manifest itself in an imperfect ability to listen, think, speak, read, write, spell, or do mathematical calculations. The term includes such conditions as perceptual handicaps, brain injury, minimal brain dysfunction, dyslexia, and developmental aphasia. The term does not include children who have learning problems which are primarily the result of visual or hearing handicaps, of mental retardation, of emotional disturbance, or of environmental, cultural, or economic disadvantage.

When the eligibility committee compared Billy Bob's evaluation with the preceding definition of "specific learning disability," they found that the results matched the definition. He displayed problems in language, reading, and arithmetic. He possessed perceptual handicaps and problems with fine and gross motor control. None of these problems could be explained by mental retardation —his IQ, at 105, was in the normal range. Emotional problems, visual or hearing deficits, or environmental, cultural, or economic disadvantages were not found to be Billy Bob's problems. All the signs of the evaluation pointed to perceptual handicaps and motor problems. Billy Bob was therefore declared eligible for special education services because of his specific learning disabilities.

Had Billy Bob's IQ fallen below 68 to 70, his handicapping conditions would probably have been identified as mentally retarded. With an IQ in this range and the other characteristics found in the evaluation, he would have matched the definition for mentally retarded described earlier in this chapter. He would still have been eligible for special services, but he would have been eligible because of his mental retardation rather than because he had specific learning disabilities.

In the preceding case, the child was found to possess only one major handicapping condition. But what happens if evaluation results indicate that a child has two or more handicapping conditions; for example, specific learning disabilities and additional emotional problems? Usually the eligibility committee will try to identify the primary handicapping condition—the condition primarily responsible for inhibiting the child's educational growth. If both conditions contribute equally to the child's learning problems, the committee may declare the child eligible for special education on the grounds of being multiply handicapped.

School systems differ significantly in the extent to which they allow parents to participate in eligibility meetings. Some permit parents to attend the meeting, present their views, bring additional witnesses, ask questions of committee members, and be present when the committee takes its final vote. At the other extreme are those school systems that fail even to notify parents when the eligibility committee is going to consider their child's case.

The procedures used by your school system should be described in your local or state regulations. Regardless of how the regulations read, or if there are none, you should ask the school officials to notify you when the eligibility committee plans to meet. You should tell them you would like to discuss your opinions with the committee and that you would like to participate with the committee as they make their decision. You should have no problem at all in getting agreement to present your opinions to the committee. On the other hand, the school system may balk at allowing you to sit with the committee as it discusses your child's case and makes its final decision. While one would hope public schools would not choose to work in such a clandestine manner, they still may do so. Federal and state laws *tend not to require* parent participation in final decisions on eligibility. The spirit of these laws, however, is one of openness and increased parent participation. Therefore, more and more school systems are opening eligibility meetings to parent participation as well as parent presentations of their opinions.

When you attend the eligibility meeting you should take the following steps:

1. At the beginning of the meeting ask the chairman what procedures will be used in the meeting, whether you may stay throughout the meeting, and what will be the final outcomes from the meeting, i.e., will a decision on eligibility be made now or later. This step is very important, since it causes everyone to proceed with the same expectations for the meeting and thus eliminates much confusion.

2. Get another person—friend, spouse, or professional—to attend the meeting with you. At the eligibility meeting you will find anywhere from four to ten school officials in attendance. If you show up alone, the meeting will tend to seem lonely and threatening. You should acquaint the person accompanying you with what you plan to do at the meeting. That person should then make sure you do what you said you would do. He or she should also be another pair of "ears" at the meeting—listening to what is going on and bringing to your attention any matters you may have missed.

3. Develop your presentation in writing so you can read or refer to it. The presentation should

   a. emphasize all the data supporting your diagnosis of your child's handi-capping condition. These data should reflect all relevant evaluations and records;
   b. describe your child's learning style as well as factors related to his or her handicapping conditions;
   c. refute or explain, where necessary, contradictory data, biases, etc.;
   d. identify the type of education and services required to meet your child's learning needs and to build on his or her learning strengths;
   e. most important, begin by passing around a picture or two of your child or even having your child briefly meet the committee. The committee should feel your child's presence at that meeting and remember there is a young boy or girl behind the records they are reviewing.

4. In many instances you may wish to bring to the meeting the professionals, teachers, and others who have worked with and know your child. Talk with them about this, find out what their opinions and views would add to your case, and then ask them to come if you think it would help. You would then develop your presentation to allow these persons to discuss their views at the appropriate times.

5. Finally, if you can stay during the committee's deliberations, listen care-fully to the committee's discussion. If committee members appear to be using biased, inaccurate, incomplete, or out-of-date material or to be making incorrect statements, intervene and explain your concerns. In all these matters remember that diplomacy and tact throughout the meeting will serve you better than angry words and shouted epithets—no matter how warranted.

70

Most of the material for your presentation should come from the analysis you made with the Four-Step Record Decoder.

POINTS OF CONTENTION
IN THE ELIGIBILITY MEETING

Two major points of contention arise between parents and school systems as a result of eligibility meetings. One problem occurs when the committee finds the child ineligible for services and the parents believe the child is eligible.* The other problem surfaces when the committee finds the child eligible but says the child's handicapping condition is something different from what the parents believe it is. An example of this second problem is when the committee concludes that a child is primarily emotionally disturbed but the parents feel the child is primarily learning disabled. Or the committee may conclude that the child is mentally retarded and the parents believe him or her to be learning disabled.

For parents and children, either of the preceding problems is serious. Therefore, parents should actively participate in the eligibility meeting and not wait for such problems to occur before entering the special education maze. By following the suggestions made to this point, you will often be able to head off these problems. And if that is accomplished, you are halfway through the maze. If either of these problems does occur, even with your active participation, you may challenge the eligibility committee's findings through a conciliatory conference or administrative review within the school system or through an impartial due process hearing. (More about these matters in Chapter 7.) *But don't forget, if your child is declared ineligible for services, or if you feel the committee has "labeled" your child incorrectly, you do not have to accept these results. You can appeal these decisions.*

A FINAL LOOK
AT EVALUATION AND ELIGIBILITY

Evaluation and eligibility determination are key phases in the special education cycle. An accurate, perceptive evaluation will pinpoint your child's specific learning problems and in many instances may identify the causes of those difficulties. A valid evaluation is essential to a fair and reliable determination of your child's eligibility to receive special education services.

*A problem could arise if the eligibility committee found a child eligible for special services but the parents refused to permit their child to receive those services. Under these conditions the school system could request a due process hearing to force the parents to allow their child to receive special education. In practice, however, if parents refuse permission for their children to receive special services, most school systems will not fight that decision through a hearing.

Evaluation results, unfortunately, do not always provide clear, precise insights into your child's learning problems and what causes them. When this happens, the eligibility meeting attains an even greater importance in your child's educational future. At this meeting, school officials will review available evaluation results, other records, and verbal testimony and make a decision regarding the meaning of this confusing information for your child's future educational placement. You cannot allow this meeting and these decisions to take place without your active participation. By following the previous suggestions for obtaining and interpreting school records, for troubleshooting evaluation, and for participating in the eligibility meeting, you will be able to exert maximum personal influence in these activities. Through these efforts you will have an active voice in your child's educational planning; if your voice is not heard, you have laid the essential groundwork for initiating a due process appeal.

Chapter 6

The Individualized
Education Program

Road Maps,
Sign Posts,
One-way Streets

INTRODUCTION

You have gained your passport to the maze! Your child has been declared eligible to receive special education services. You spent a lot of time and energy preparing to reach this place. You took a close look at your child's growth and development from two points of view, your own and the school system's.

As you formulated your own point of view, you observed your child, noting things he recently learned or accomplished. You sharpened your awareness of behavior he is attempting, of tasks he is trying to accomplish. Next you looked ahead, down the road. Targets were set for behavior and learning you hope your child might accomplish in the not-too-distant future. All of this information, your valuable perspective as a parent, you then organized on the Developmental Achievement Chart under the headings of *Can Do, Working On,* and *To Accomplish within Six Months.*

The second point of view, that is, the school system's, you acquired by obtaining and analyzing written records about your child. In these records you found test results, observations, and recommendations of teachers, psychologists, therapists, physicians, and other professional persons. You wrote down their recommendations on matters such as the type of appropriate classroom, the ratio of students to teachers in the classroom, the kind of related services needed, and other specific requirements. By using the Four-Step Record Decoder you noted strengths, problems, and descriptions of your child's learning style. By organizing and analyzing his records, you found trends and consistencies corresponding to your own observations and to the experience you have gained from the many years of living with your child.

This carefully prepared information formed the basis for your participation in the eligibility committee meeting. (As mentioned in Chapter 5, various states have different names for this committee. For example, in one state it is called Admission Review and Dismissal (ARD) Committee, while in another it is called the Placement Committee.) Whatever the committee is named, its function is the same—it is required to reach a decision with regard to your child's eligibility for special education services. In the eligibility meeting you presented the information you worked carefully to prepare, and in this way assisted the committee in reaching its decision. If the outcome was a recommendation for your child to receive special education services, you now will turn a corner into another corridor of the special education maze. In this corridor you will again use your written materials to provide information for planning your child's Individualized Education Program, or IEP.

WHAT IS AN IEP?

An Individualized Education Program (IEP) is two things—a written planning document and a meeting. In the first half of this chapter you will find a description of the IEP document. The five required parts of an IEP are outlined with examples illustrating ways in which parents can contribute and have contributed to each of the parts. The second half of the chapter deals with the IEP meeting. Who participates in the IEP meeting? Is the document to be written beforehand by the teacher, waiting only for parents' approval? What role or roles are parents to take in the planning meeting for a student's school program?

THE IEP WRITTEN DOCUMENT

The Individualized Education Program (IEP) planning document is a written program tailored to fit the unique educational needs of your child. In the business world one hears of management by objectives. In the school world, the IEP is a plan of management by objectives for your child's educational program. This management system is planned jointly by parents, educators, and on many occasions the person for whom the plans are being made, *your child.* Objectives for the student are outlined and must be agreeable to all parties involved in the planning and provision of services. The educational setting in which the objectives will be reached, when the services will begin, how long they will last, and the ways in which the student will be measured in the accomplishment of the program are included in the IEP. Once again, your home observations and the record decoding provide valuable information for your work with educators to write your child's IEP.

IEP PART 1:
A DESCRIPTION OF THE STUDENT

The first component of the IEP answers the question, "Who is this child?". After all, everyone involved in his education must come to know the person described in the written program. The usual information, such as name, age, address, and other identifying factors, is included. This section of the IEP also contains a description of your child as he is right now. It shows his current level of educational and behavioral performance. On the IEP document this information is written in a box or space labeled *Present Level of Functioning and Academic Performance,* or simply *Present Level,* or anything similar, depending upon your local school system's format.

Where have parents collected information necessary to contribute to the student's present level of performance? In Chapter 2, Strengthening Exercise #3, the Developmental Achievement Chart, you filled out a column labeled *Can Do* in each of the developmental areas. In Chapter 4, in the Four-Step Record Decoder, you recorded strengths and accomplishments in each developmental area. The *Can Do* and *Strengths* are the information sources for your child's present level of functioning. The following chart presents examples parents have gathered from each source.

DEVELOPMENTAL ACHIEVEMENT CHART	*FOUR-STEP RECORD DECODER*
Can Do	*Strengths*
set the table completely and correctly for four persons	is able to follow two commands
catch the bus, transfer to the subway, and get to school on time	knows the multiplication table through the 5s
follow a recipe to bake a cake	consistently uses "m" sound to indicate need for "more"
roll over from front to back	on Peabody Individual Achievement Test (PIAT)
skip rope when others turn the rope	Reading recog. 2.3 gr. level
	Reading comp. 1.6 gr. level
	Math 2.0 gr. level
	can use a head pointer on the typewriter to spell individual words

In IEP Part 1 you have the opportunity to contribute your very important information about your child's unique learning style. Be sure to include written descriptions of your child's way of approaching a learning situation. The ways in which your child learns best can take a new teacher weeks or months to discover. You can help the teacher and your child avoid some frustrations by including in the "present level" such descriptions as:

- He needs a quiet, secluded place for concentrated work.
- She learns quickly when working in a small group of children.
- He understands and learns better what he hears rather than what he sees.
- She imitates other children and learns from them.

These descriptions of *Can Do, Strengths,* and *Learning Style* are the substance of the first part of the IEP. Listing numerical attainment such as 4th grade, IQ 94, or age equivalent of three years is insufficient. Descriptive statements are required in order for all persons involved in teaching your child to know him. The present level of performance is the foundation upon which the second part of the IEP is built.

IEP PART 2:
GOALS AND OBJECTIVES

In the second section of the IEP, goals and objectives are written to point toward those accomplishments or behaviors you believe your child should attain. Before thinking about goals and objectives for your particular child, a look at the process of setting goals is in order. We set goals for ourselves and for others all the time. What are goals? Simply stated, goals are long-range plans. As adults, as parents, you make long-range plans for a number of things. You might set a goal to buy a new car, to lose ten pounds, to take a family vacation, to plant a vegetable garden. You make plans for what you would like to do, for what is important to your family. Within each of these plans some decisions must be made. To plan a vacation you might consider:

Who will go with you? The whole family? Should we invite the grandparents?
What will you do? Go camping? Visit relatives? Swim in the ocean?
How will you get there? By car? By bus?
Where will you go? To the mountains? To the beach?
When will you go and *how long* will you stay? Early summer? Late summer? To stay forever?

After you and your family have made these decisions, you could write a goal for your vacation plans.

Goal: My family will drive to the mountains to camp for one week beginning August 4.

This goal for a family vacation contains five necessary ingredients or parts. It answers *who?* will do *what? how? where?* and *when?* These five basic parts are necessary for all goals.

In order to reach the goal of the family camping vacation, many smaller specific plans must be made. You choose a state park to camp in, arrange annual leave from your job, borrow a tent, find a kennel for Rover, and take many other interim steps to make it possible to go to the mountains. These smaller plans are objectives.

IEP goals and objectives are much the same as described above. Goals are long-range plans; objectives are the intermediate steps necessary to reach the long-range goals. The annual goals written on an IEP state what your child is expected to do in one year. Each goal must be written as:

1. a positive statement that . . .
2. describes an observable event.

A well-written goal not only tells what skill your child will achieve, but also is written in such a way that you and others can observe the achievement. You have to be able to *see* or to *hear* what he has learned to do in order to know if he is making progress. Many IEPs contain faulty goals whose outcomes are not observable or measurable.

> *Poorly Written Goals*
> Bonnie Jean will improve her self-concept.
> Edward will communicate better.
> Jamie will grow stronger.
> Kevin will learn to write.
> Nina will be cooperative.

None of these poorly written goals fulfills both criteria of being (1) a positive statement that (2) describes an observable skill. None of these poorly written goals contains all five essential parts.

> Who? . . . . . will achieve?
> What? . . . . skill or behavior?
> How? . . . . in what manner or at what level?
> Where? . . . in what setting or under what conditions?
> When? . . . . by what time? an ending date?

A well-written goal contains all five parts.

> *Well-Written Goals*
> Edward will use self-help words, appropriately using sign language in his classroom and speech therapy by June 30.
> Nina will prepare and present an oral report in social studies with two regular education classmates by May 7.

Each of these well-written goals is a positive statement describing an observable skill. They each answer the questions of who? will do what? how? where? and when? With goals and objectives written carefully and specifically, you and everyone else involved in teaching your child will hold the same expectations for him.

Objectives are intermediate steps taken to reach the long-range goal. Just as there are specific interim tasks necessary to make your vacation run smoothly, there are small steps or accomplishments your child needs to take in order to reach the annual goals written on his IEP. Short-term objectives are the steps to be taken between the "present level of performance" and the "annual goal." Short-term objectives contain the same five basic parts as annual goals—the who, what, how, where, and when.

An example of a well-written goal, based upon the present level of performance, with appropriate short-term objectives, is found below. This goal, written by Jamie's parents and teacher, is in the developmental category of movement.

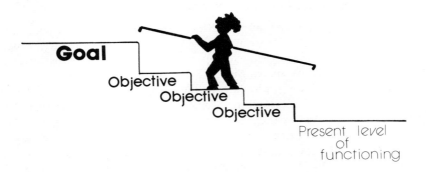

ANNUAL GOAL   Jamie will walk upstairs, using one foot per tread, without assistance, at home and at school, by June 1.

PRESENT LEVEL OF PERFORMANCE   Jamie walks steadily on flat ground, but goes up the stairs on his hands and knees.

OBJECTIVE 1   Jamie will walk upstairs with two feet per tread, holding the handrail and an adult's hand, by October 15.

OBJECTIVE 2   Jamie will walk upstairs with two feet per tread holding only the handrail by December 1.

OBJECTIVE 3   Jamie will walk upstairs one foot per tread holding the handrail and an adult's hand by March 15.

The goal and each of the objectives fulfill the requirements for well-written goals and objectives. They describe milestones for Jamie's accomplishment that can be observed within a specific time frame as he works toward the goal of climbing stairs unassisted.

Many questions arise as parents think about goals and objectives for their child.

1. *How can I know if a goal is reasonable to expect of my child? Does it demand too much or not enough of him?*

The answer to this question lies in part with the IEP meeting. A group of people, knowledgeable of the child (parents, present and former teachers, other specialists) and knowledgeable of child development and handicapping conditions are brought together to discuss reasonable expectations. Goals are set while looking at present levels of performance, at the rate your child has been developing thus far, and at the sequence and timing of normal growth and development. These considerations are helpful in setting appropriate goals and short-term objectives. You, or the teacher, do not have to do this task of setting goals and objectives alone. A group works together.

2. *Should goals and objectives be written for all aspects of his education?*

Goals and objectives are required for all special education services. If your child has been declared eligible for speech therapy or a special adapted physical education program, there must be goals and objectives written in each specialized area. "Bonnie Jean will receive speech therapy" or "Bonnie Jean will be in adaptive P.E." are not acceptable ways to describe the services. Goals must be written to describe what she will accomplish in language or physical development. For example, if Bonnie Jean's present level of performance in language describes her use of two-word phrases, an example of a goal might be: "Bonnie Jean will speak in three-word sentences using noun, verb, object construction in the classroom and speech therapy by May 15." This goal, built on her present level of functioning, serves to alert all teachers and her parents to work consistently toward the next step in her growth in communication skills.

3. *Must there be goals and objectives written on the IEP for the parts of his program in the regular education classroom?*

Generally, goals and objectives are required only for special education services. They cover those areas of development in which your child has special problems. A very clear requirement, however, is for the regular education classroom teacher to have a copy of the IEP, or at the very least to be informed of its content. The school system must allow the special educator or specialist time to consult or provide assistance needed to the regular classroom teacher. In this way, all teachers work consistently toward the same goals.

4. *Is it necessary for parents to develop knowledge and skills to write goals and objectives, knowing this skill is taught in schools of education and knowing it can take teachers a long time to acquire mastery in this area?*

Some parents have found they are able to acquire this skill by understanding the essential requirements for writing goals and objectives and by applying this to their particular child. Other parents prefer to leave the actual writing of goals and objectives to the educators, but are careful to know in which developmental areas they feel their child needs special attention. They are able to be specific about the directions toward which to point the goals. Knowing how goals and objectives are structured, they are able to critique and offer suggestions concerning the goals and objectives written by the educators. In either case, the better your understanding of the nature of goals and objectives and of your child's abilities and problems, the more effective you will be as a member of the educational planning team. With your help, the goals and objectives written very specifically for your child's needs allow you and his teachers to assess his rate of growth and his developmental progress.

IEP PART 3:
SPECIAL EDUCATION SERVICES

It is all well and good to have specific goals and objectives for your child—but goals and objectives are not enough! Next come decisions concerning placement. Where, or in what educational setting, can these goals and objectives best be met by your child? In years past children with special education needs have been placed in classrooms solely on the basis of *disability* groupings. For example, children with physical disabilities such as cerebral palsy, or children able to move about only with the help of a wheelchair, would be placed in classrooms in which all students had physical disabilities. Similarly, students who had learning problems associated with Down's Syndrome or other mental retardation were automatically grouped with students with the same disabilities. The IEP requirements call for changes in the ways of grouping children. The IEP focuses the attention of parents, teachers, administrators and therapists on *ability* as well as on disability. Everyone looks at the child's learning strengths and problems. Goals and objectives are formulated in order to use the student's learning strengths to overcome or compensate for the disabilities. Only after these goals and objectives are carefully prepared and careful study is made of the specific educational needs of a student is a placement recommended. Part 3 of the IEP is the description of special education and related services to be provided and the amount of participation in the regular education classroom. Clearly, the intent of PL 94–142 is to determine a student's placement only after the IEP goals and objectives have been worked out mutually with parents, educators, and, very often, the student. Placement is made on the basis of the strengths and needs of the student, by choosing a learning environment in which the educational goals and objectives can best be carried out.

But, you ask, on what criteria is this decision based? Two equally important factors must be weighed and balanced as you participate in making the placement decision.

1. the appropriate educational program
2. the least restrictive environment

The words of the Education for All Handicapped Children Act herald these two provisions which are the heart of the new opportunities for our nation's handicapped children.

> It is the purpose of this Act to assure that all handicapped children have available to them . . . a free appropriate public education which emphasizes special education and related services designed to meet their unique needs.
> To the maximum extent appropriate, handicapped children, including children in public or private institutions or other care facilities, are educated with children who are not handicapped.

The planning activities you have undertaken thus far as you have traveled the special education maze through evaluation, eligibility, and the development of goals and objectives for the IEP point you toward appropriate services. To determine the extent to which your child will be educated with children who are not handicapped, that is, to determine the *least restrictive placement* for your child, the following chart provides assistance. Evelyn Deno, in *Educating Children with Emotional, Learning and Behavioral Problems,** has drawn a diagram to describe the various combinations of services which are required by students in special education.

The tapered design is used to indicate the considerable difference in numbers of children likely to be involved at the different levels of service. At the top of the chart is the least restrictive setting for a student in a special education program. At this level, he spends all day in the regular classroom with supportive services provided either within that classroom or in a therapy setting. Moving down the cascade, you find the handicapped child spending more of his time with other students who are also handicapped. The most specialized, most restrictive facilities are needed by the fewest number of children. This diagram provides an easy and beneficial guide for parents and educators to use as they seek to determine the educational placement for a child which is both educationally appropriate and least restrictive.

To use the cascade system, a parent begins at the top of the diagram and asks, "Is the regular classroom, or the regular classroom with support services, the learning environment in which my child's goals and objectives will best be met?" Included in this type of special education are many children who in past years might have been excluded from participation in the regular classroom with

---

*Evelyn N. Deno, *Educating Children with Emotional Learning and Behavior Problems* (Minneapolis, Minn.: University of Minnesota, Leadership Training Institute/Special Education, 1978), p. 109.

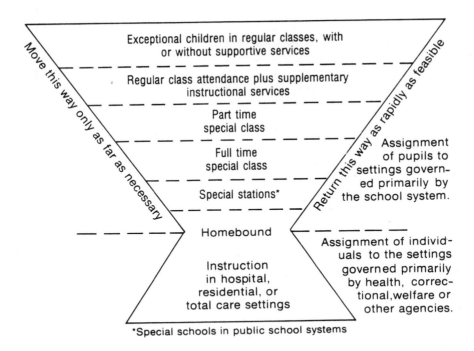

Exceptional children in regular classes, with
or without supportive services

Regular class attendance plus supplementary
instructional services

Part time
special class

Full time
special class

Special stations*

Homebound

Instruction
in hospital,
residential, or
total care settings

Move this way only as far as necessary

Return this way as rapidly as feasible

Assignment
of pupils to
settings govern-
ed primarily by
the school system.

Assignment of individ-
uals to the settings
governed primarily
by health, correc-
tional, welfare or
other agencies.

*Special schools in public school systems

nonhandicapped children. For example, Juanita uses a walker for support as she moves about. In previous years she was assigned to a classroom for orthopedically handicapped children because that classroom was located on the ground level. This year, however, her goals and objectives indicate regular classroom placement with the supportive service of physical therapy twice a week. The school building in which she will attend eighth grade now has ramps available for her to move to various levels of the building. Juanita's program was based on both factors:

1. *The appropriate educational program:* The IEP goals and objectives include physical milestones to be reached, academic achievements, and social/emotional growth. She will receive support service of physical therapy for thirty minutes twice a week to assist in her physical development.

2. *The least restrictive environment:* Juanita's goals and objectives can be realized in the regular education program, which provides maximum time for Juanita in a classroom with children who are not handicapped. For only one hour each week will she be separated from her 8th-grade classmates, for physical therapy.

In every special education placement for *every* child, the appropriate education and the least restrictive environment must be given equal consideration. Many people in many places have misinterpreted the least restrictive environment to mean that all children with disabilities will be dumped into the mainstream, or regular education classroom. The least restrictive environment concept must always be coupled with what is appropriate education for each individual child. For Sally, a child who needs instruction in feeding herself, in learning to sit or crawl, in basic self-care, the appropriate education in the least restrictive setting might be in a special class all day or even in a residential school. For this child, the appropriate education requires very specialized instruction not available in a regular classroom. The maximum extent of her involvement with children who are not handicapped might be with peer tutors from regular classrooms. Other contact with nonhandicapped students might come from her attendance at auditorium programs, special music classes, and daily lunch in the lunchroom.

Deno's cascade system of special education services enables parents and school personnel to plan carefully for each child's services. By moving down the diagram only as far as necessary for appropriate education, each handicapped child can be assured of education in the least restrictive environment.

Below are three examples of special education placements planned for children in the IEP meeting. Look at Deno's cascade of services and decide at which level each of these is served.

EXAMPLE 1   Robert will be in the regular education classroom throughout the school day. The itinerant teacher for children with visual handicaps will provide talking books, consultation with the teacher about classroom adaptations, and individualized prescriptive teaching on a one-to-one basis for Robert.

EXAMPLE 2   Martha's reading, arithmetic, spelling, and handwriting goals will be met in the learning disabilities resource classroom. She will participate in social studies, science, music, and art in the third-grade regular education classroom. Special physical education will be provided by a teacher for the physically handicapped.

EXAMPLE 3   Claudia attends a special school for her academic training and her self-care skills. Her program includes vocational training in homemaking, gardening, and food service.

In addition to the classroom setting for your child's special education program, the IEP describes related services to be provided. These services might include one or more of the following:

> occupational therapy
> vocational education
> social work services
> medical diagnosis/evaluation
> audiological training

recreation
adaptive physical education
counseling/parent training
speech/language therapy
transportation
psychological services

In the same way that present level of performance, goals, objectives, and classroom placement are individually determined for students, so, too, are related or supportive services. Your child is guaranteed those related services necessary for him to benefit from special education. One might argue that every child in special education would stand to gain from receiving maximum attention from a number of highly trained specialists. This argument circles back to the question of the least restrictive placement. If a student is taken out of his classroom several times a day by various support service specialists, his day becomes fragmented, his need for continuity with a group of classmates unmet. Therefore, only those related services necessary to help him benefit from his educational program are to be provided for him. The regulations*   for PL94–142 define each related service as follows:

Audiology
1. identification of children with hearing loss;
2. determination of the range, nature, and degree of hearing loss, including referral for medical or other professional attention for the habilitation of hearing;
3. provision of habilitative activities, such as language habilitation, auditory training, speech reading (lipreading), hearing evaluation, and speech conservation;
4. creation and administration of programs for prevention of hearing loss;
5. counseling and guidance of pupils, parents, and teachers regarding hearing loss; and
6. determination of the child's need for group and individual amplification, selecting and fitting an appropriate aid, and evaluating the effectiveness of amplification.

Counseling Services
Services provided by qualified social workers, psychologists, guidance counselors, or other qualified personnel.

Early Identification
The implementation of a formal plan for identifying a disability as early as possible in a child's life.

*Federal Register 42, No. 163, 23 August 1977.

Medical Services
Services provided by a licensed physician to determine a child's medically related handicapping condition which results in the child's need for special education and related services.

Occupational Therapy
1. improving, developing, or restoring functions impaired or lost through illness, injury, or deprivation;
2. improving ability to perform tasks for independent functioning when functions are impaired or lost; and
3. preventing, through early intervention, initial or further impairment or loss of function.

Parent Counseling and Training
Assisting parents in understanding the special needs of their child and providing parents with information about child development.

Physical Therapy
Services provided by a qualified physical therapist.

Psychological Services
1. administering psychological and educational tests, and other assessment procedures;
2. interpreting assessment results;
3. obtaining, integrating, and interpreting information about child behavior and conditions relating to learning;
4. consulting with other staff members in planning school programs to meet the special needs of children as indicated by psychological tests, interviews, and behavioral evaluations; and
5. planning and managing a program of psychological services, including psychological counseling for children and parents.

Recreation
1. assessment of leisure function;
2. therapeutic recreation services;
3. recreation programs in schools and community agencies; and
4. leisure education.

School Health Services
Services provided by a qualified school nurse or other qualified person.

Social Work Services
1. preparing a social or developmental history on a handicapped child;
2. group and individual counseling with the child and family;
3. working with those problems in a child's living situation (home, school, and community) that affect the child's adjustment in school; and

4. mobilizing school and community resources to enable the child to receive maximum benefit from his or her educational program.

Speech Pathology
1. identification of children with speech or language disorders;
2. diagnosis and appraisal of specific speech or language disorders;
3. referral for medical or other professional attention necessary for the habilitation of speech or language disorders;
4. provisions of speech and language services for the habilitation or prevention of communicative disorders; and
5. counseling and guidance of parents, children, and teachers regarding speech and language disorders.

Transportation
1. travel to and from school and between schools;
2. travel in and around school buildings; and
3. specialized equipment (such as special or adapted buses, lifts, and ramps), if required to provide special transportation for a handicapped child.

Many questions occur as you read the list of possible services the school might provide for your child. What kinds of services are needed? How often? For what length of time each day or week? Who will provide the services? How can you determine answers to the above questions? Who are the decision-makers? Parents? School administrators? Outside experts? School boards? Teachers? As these questions are considered by parents and educators in the placement decision, you will find there are no easy answers. Many questions arise.

Question 1: Are the services to be provided for my child only those currently available in our school system?

Question 2: With school budgets tightening each year, is there any way to provide additional services needed by my child?

Question 3: If required services are not available within the school system, must they be purchased by the school system from other agencies or individuals?

Question 4: If I push too hard for this, will I alienate the people whose cooperation I need for the well-being of my child?

Question 5: How do I know/determine what is appropriate for my child?

Question 6: Even when I feel sure these special services are required for my child, what if the providers of such services don't live in my community?

Question 7: Related and support services are important, but how do I evaluate the importance of these, balanced against my child's need for a consistent program with his teacher and classmates in the educational classroom? I don't want his program to be too fragmented.

Question 8: Are the related service providers available to work in the regular or special education classroom rather than taking my child off to an isolated therapy setting?

Question 9: Do the therapists and teachers talk with one another about goals/objectives so that there is consistency in my child's program?

Question 10: If I disagree with the services proposed by the school system, will going to a due process hearing, even if I win, actually provide what my child needs?

Question 11: What is the best way to bring about change for my child in the kinds and quality of support services?

As you have discovered, the more information you have collected and the more knowledgeable you are for each stage in the special education maze, the better able you are to make your views known to key decision-makers. In the determination of related services, this applies once again. A resource list appears in Appendix C, where literature on related services is available. For example, *The American Alliance for Health, Physical Education, Recreation and Dance* has materials available to parents on the special physical education requirements of children. Valuable guidance can come from this group to assist you in negotiating physical education services. Likewise, the *American Speech and Hearing Association* can provide guidelines for parents as they consider their child's requirement for speech and language therapy. Ask questions of specialists, discuss your child's need for related services with physicians, talk to other parents whose children seem to require similar services. After you accumulate information from a variety of sources, you will be able to weigh and balance the needs of your child, the needs of the school system, and the available service providers. In this way you will determine your priorities for your child's supportive services as you prepare for and participate in the IEP meeting.

IEP PART 4:
TIME AND DURATION OF SERVICES

You have moved through three stops along the IEP corridor in the special education maze. The fourth stop guarantees you won't get stuck in one place. In this section the time and timing for your child's program are determined. Once the goals and objectives are written and the services decided upon, the school system has a duty to begin these services without undue delay. Most states specify the number of days within which a program must begin following parents' signing permission for the program. At no time is a child to wait at home for special education services to begin, unless an agreement has been reached between you and the school system for a temporary homebound program. Occasionally conditions call for a temporary placement, to which parents and the school system must agree, if a child endangers himself or others by remaining in the former placement.

Under ordinary circumstances, a date is determined in the IEP meeting for the beginning of the services. In addition, the expected duration for these services is recorded. The expected duration might be six weeks for a support service of counseling with a social worker, to be followed by an assessment of progress and a recommendation for either continuing this service or ending it. Or the expected duration may be a year at a time for such parts of the program as classroom placement. Because of the requirement of an annual review of the services provided in the IEP, the long-term duration for services should be projected no further than one year. The annual review ensures that no child will be left in special education with no careful overview of his changing needs. Once each year an evaluation is made of the appropriateness of the special education services and of the least restrictive environment for each child.

Along with the long-term duration, many IEP forms call for "duration of service" to indicate short-term, daily hours. For example, Jessica will attend speech therapy twice a week, on Monday and Thursday, from 10:00 to 10:30. Certainly parents will want to get specific information on the times and timing of all of the parts of the school program for their child. Too often children who have special services miss some of the most important parts of the instruction in the classroom. For example, when Willie went to the learning disabilities resource room for special instruction in math, he missed his reading group in the regular education classroom. He was falling behind in reading until his parents talked to his regular class teacher and the resource room teacher. As a result both teachers adjusted their schedules in order to accommodate his instruction in reading and math.

IEP PART 5:
WAYS OF EVALUATING THE IEP

Parents and teachers periodically need to determine if short-term objectives are being met. In other words, how do you know if your child is making progress? The critical element in evaluation comes in writing clear, measurable, observable goals and objectives. When such a goal is written as "Suzy will improve self-esteem," parents and teachers will be hard pressed to know when and how Suzy has arrived at this improved state of well-being. A specific annual goal for Suzy might be, "Suzy will demonstrate pleasure in her own accomplishments by planning and completing classroom projects on time by June 30," and a short-term objective might be, "Suzy will choose two classmates, with whom she will cooperatively plan and complete an art project to illustrate a story in the fifth-level reader by January 14." To evaluate the objective, parents and teachers might ask the following questions:

1. Was the art project completed on time?
2. Did Suzy read and comprehend the story?

3. Did the teacher observe and note incidents to illustrate Suzy's cooperation with classmates?
4. What indications show that Suzy made plans for the project? What were the media chosen? Who took responsibility for what parts of the project?
5. In what ways did Suzy demonstrate pleasure in her accomplishments? Did she urge her parents to come to open house to see it? Was she eager to show and tell about the project?

A specific goal or objective such as the ones written for Suzy allows parents and teachers to ask critical questions pertaining to Suzy's growth and development. When Suzy completes the objective, one could guess that she would indeed have good feelings about her school work, about her relationship to her classmates, and about herself.

At least once a year, and at any other time when either a teacher or parent requests it, a meeting is held to review progress toward goals and objectives. Very often in the space on the IEP for "objective criteria and evaluation procedures," you see written "teacher-made tests" or "teacher assessment." You may wish to inquire about these tests. What will they be? When will they be given? Are there other ways of measuring progress? Tape recorders, examples of school-work, classroom observations, completed projects, standardized tests, and many other techniques are useful in evaluation. By using information from a variety of sources, the teaching team comprised of teachers, specialists, and parents together can measure progress in a student's growth and learning.

A PLANNING CHART FOR THE IEP

Now that you have gone past the five stops in the IEP corridor, you may wish to complete the following chart to prepare for the upcoming IEP meeting. You will concentrate on those areas of development in which your child has particular problems and needs special services to help in overcoming or compensating for those problems. In column A write a brief description of the problem, followed by the "Present Level of Functioning" in column B. Columns C and D are spaces for your ideas for long-range goals and short-term objectives to help your child with the problem. In column E you can write the place or places in the school program where you believe these objectives can most suitably be worked on. Column F is a place for you to put ideas for checking progress on the goals and objectives. Following the blank chart included for your use, you will find an example of an IEP Planning Chart filled out by Sara's parents before they attended her IEP meeting. A sample of Sara's IEP is found on pages 95 and 96.

INDIVIDUALIZED EDUCATION PROGRAM PLANNING CHART

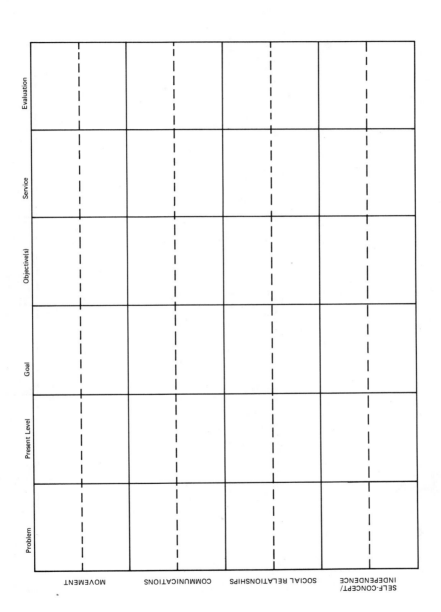

	Problem	Present Level	Goal	Objective(s)	Service	Evaluation
MOVEMENT						
COMMUNICATIONS						
SOCIAL RELATIONSHIPS						
SELF-CONCEPT/INDEPENDENCE						

INDIVIDUALIZED EDUCATION PROGRAM PLANNING CHART

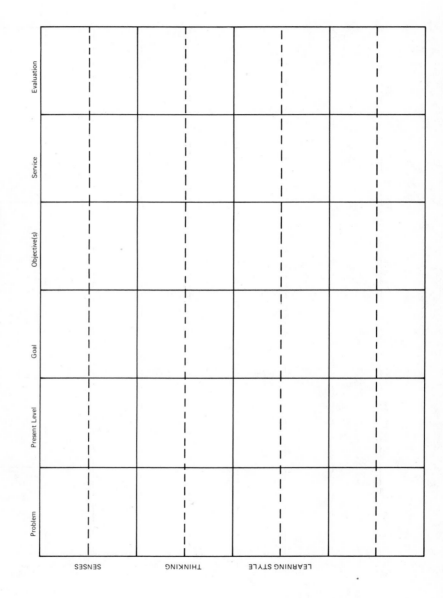

	Problem	Present Level	Goal	Objective(s)	Service	Evaluation
SENSES						
THINKING						
LEARNING STYLE						

	Problem	Present Level	Goal	Objective(s)	Service	Evaluation
MOVEMENT	Poor motor planning	She gives up in the middle of an obstacle course	to find her way across an obstacle course	1) Practice skills for individual sections to do on entire course 2) Understand what to do on entire course	Adaptive P.E.	By June 30 she will complete obstacle course unassisted
	Trouble drawing complicated human figures	Draws simple shapes and people (figures)	to draw more complex figures in a recognizable way	1) Draw shapes using a stencil 2) Draw shapes without stencil - and on pictures	Special ed. Classroom and regular ed. art classes	By June 30 Dana's human figure drawings will include 10 specific parts
COMMUNICATIONS	Poor word finding skills	Forgets names of common household items - hairbrush, toothbrush, radio	to increase her retrieval skills	1) work with vocabulary words 2) use real words correctly & spontaneously	Special ed. classroom	Tape recorded conversations
	Poor sequencing skills	Talks about daily activities with no attention to the proper order	To tell about her day or weekend in sequential order	1) Dana will talk about single experiences 2) she will keep an activity calendar	Speech/language therapy	Tape recording compare with 9/11 tape
SOCIAL RELATIONSHIPS	Frequently tells peers what to do - wants her own way	Bossily tells friends play Barbie dolls or the way they want play	With a classmate she will plan a project in a "give and take" way	1) plan with friend under staff direction and praise 2) work with classmate independently	Special ed. Classroom	Anecdotal notes of sp ed teacher
	Makes negative comments about herself when she makes mistakes	she says "I hate myself" when she does something wrong	Dana will praise herself verbally for a job well done	1) she will show something positive when reprimanded 2) imitate a shoulder shrug when she makes mistakes	All teachers + family	Anecdotal notes
SELF-CONCEPT/ INDEPENDENCE	She feels different	Asks why she is in special classes and her sister is not	Dana will describe ways she is same/different from a friend	1) Describe same/different clothing 2) Identify same/different personality traits	Special ed. and reg. ed. classes and at home with family + friends	Teacher and parent observations
	Extreme need for nurturance	Sits and waits alone on front porch for long periods if Mom is not home on time	To make make independent decision to go to neighbor's when she gets home from bus alone	1) Make a chart recording plan for alone time 2) Explain plan to neighbor + teacher	Sp. ed. teacher home & neighbor	Parent observation - chart completed

INDIVIDUALIZED EDUCATION PROGRAM PLANNING CHART

	Problem	Present Level	Goal	Objective(s)	Service	Evaluation
SENSES	Doesn't remember details of pictures	Remembers vaguely the whole picture without studying details	To look at picture and describe more than two details	1) Identify missing details of picture by drawing them in. 2) Look and tell name missing details	Sp. ed. classroom	Oral test
	Difficulty following multiple oral directions	Follows one direction at a time	To carry out directions given three at a time	1) Follows one command correctly 2) Repeat directions aloud before acting	Sp. ed. classroom speech therapy home	Informal teacher made tests
THINKING	Disorganized way of describing a story she's read	Tells about a story in generalized way - no attention to proper order	To understand and tell main ideas in short stories	1) describe main characters 2) describe one event 3) decide on main idea	Sp. ed. classroom and book report time	By time, she will present an oral book report and accurately tell the main idea
	Does not understand the value of coins	Confuses nickels, dimes and quarters - both value and name	To buy something and count the change	1) learn the name and value of each coin 2) count money with mixed change	Sp. ed. classroom	Demonstrate use of money
LEARNING STYLE	Haphazard planning	Leaves one homework subject to start another, then leaves both unfinished	To plan alone how to do her school work	1) with adult help she will learn to break tasks into small steps 2) make her own charts	Sp. ed. classroom	Completed planning checks - showing accomplishment
	Very concrete - not able to be abstract in thinking	Doesn't understand jokes or puns that are the least bit subtle	To learn to tell a joke	1) read a riddle - explain meaning to teacher 2) tell riddle from memory	Speech/language therapy	Tell the class a joke or riddle

Student Name Sara Austin DOB 10/8/72
Student ID# 72348   Queensbury School
Current Assignment
4th grade

INDIVIDUAL EDUCATIONAL PLAN

EXCEPTIONAL EDUCATION ASSIGNMENT(S):	INITIATION DATE	ANTICIPATED DURATION	PERSON RESPONSIBLE
Self contained noncategorical special education classroom 85% of time/week	9/82	6/83	Ms. Roberta Chase
Queensbury School			
(Location / Program / Organization / Time)			

RELATED SERVICES:

Speech and language therapy ½ hr. 3x/week	9/82	6/83	Ms. Phyllis Find
Occupational therapy ½ hr. 2x/week	9/82	6/83	

EXTENT TO WHICH STUDENT WILL PARTICIPATE IN BASIC OR VOCATIONAL
EDUCATION: __15% in basic education program__

USE OF DOUBLE BASIC COST FACTOR FOR FULL-TIME STUDENTS:
(Specify required special aids, services, or equipment)

N.A.

Subject	hours/% of time	Subject	hours/% of time
P.E.	2½ hrs./week	art	1 hr./week
Music	1 hr./week		
Vocational Education			
Physical Education X Regular ____ Adaptive			

IN ATTENDANCE AT IEP MEETING:

	Signature	Date	Signature	Date
LEA Representative (Title: Principal____)	Glen Collins		Robert Austin	9/5
Parent(s), Guardian(s) or Surrogate Parent(s)	Linda Austin	9/5		
Student	Anna Chase	9/5		
Teacher(s)				
Evaluator(s)				
Other(s)				

95

Student Name Sara Austin
Student ID# 72348
Exceptional Education Assignment

PERFORMANCE OR SUBJECT AREA: Math

PRESENT LEVEL: Adds and subtracts 2 digit numbers
Knows multiplication table through 8's
Identifies penny, but confuses nickels, dimes, quarters

ANNUAL GOAL:
Sara will be able to make change for a dollar using pennies, nickels, dimes and quarters by June.

EVALUATION OF SHORT-TERM INSTRUCTIONAL OBJECTIVES

SHORT-TERM INSTRUCTIONAL OBJECTIVES	Criterion for Mastery	Evaluation Procedures and Schedule to be used	Results/Date
1. Sara will discriminate between the 4 different coins	Accurately name the coins-- 100%	Teacher observation using real coins by Oct. 29	
2. Sara will identify the coin and its value	Write number value under picture of coin	Worksheets on coins completed accurately in independent work by Jan. 1	
3. Sara will make change for a dime in three ways.	Demonstrate with real coins	Teacher observation by March 1	
4. Sara will make change for a quarter in three ways.	Use pennies, nickels and dimes to make a quarter accurately-- 100%	Teacher observation by April 6	
5. Sara will purchase a box of crayons at school store and count change.	Purchase completed with 100% accuracy	Pencil and correct change given to teacher by May 27	

NOTE: Additional performance or subject area pages would be completed for Sara Austin's IEP

Once your planning is done, you will be well prepared to attend the IEP meeting. You will be able to offer valuable insights into your child's growth and development and his or her style of learning as you and the educators prepare the IEP document. The following section offers hints on how to get ready for the meeting, and also ways in which you might conduct yourself once you are there. IEP meetings come at least once a year; more often if a teacher or parent requests an interim meeting. Each time you are notified of an IEP meeting, you may want to reread this section to decide which suggestions, among the many made, you will want to carry out as you get ready for the meeting.

SOME THOUGHTS ON PREPARING FOR AND PARTICIPATING IN AN IEP MEETING

Considerations Prior to the IEP Meeting

1. Upon notification of the IEP meeting, call the person who is to direct the meeting and find out (a) who will be attending the meeting, if that information is not included in the notification, and (b) how long the meeting is scheduled to last.

2. If you believe someone providing services to your child has not been invited to the meeting, ask that he or she be invited. If he cannot attend, make arrangments to meet with him and obtain his ideas to include in the final IEP document. The minimum number of people required to be at an IEP meeting is *three:* a representative of the public school qualified to provide or supervise the provision of special education, a teacher, and a parent. Other individuals may be invited by the parents or the school system. Your child can be included if you feel it is appropriate.

3. If you feel the time allotted for the IEP meeting is too short, make arrangements to meet a second time in order to conclude the IEP meeting; or arrange to make the first meeting longer.

4. Using your personal observations, the Record Decoder, and the IEP Planning Chart for developing goals, objectives, and evaluation criteria, make notes on all of the above items you want included on the IEP, or design your own IEP to take with you to the IEP meeting.

5. Rank order the goals and objectives you want your child to achieve.

6. Talk with other persons—teachers, parents, professionals, and so on—about the special education and related services they feel your child needs. Identify

and write down in rank order the special education and related services you want your child to receive.

7. Determine the extent to which you feel your child should participate in regular education programs in light of the child's learning style and special education needs.

8. Develop these IEP elements, the rank ordering of goals and objectives, the participation in the regular education program, and the rank order of special education and related services you want your child to receive into a written agenda of concerns to be discussed at the IEP meeting.

9. Where school officials are working with your child for the first time, develop a plan for making your child's presence felt at the IEP meeting. Ensure that presence is created at the beginning of the meeting. Photographs of your family, tape recordings, examples of schoolwork, telling a short anecdote, or bringing your child can help people unacquainted with him realize that he is far more than a stack of papers!

10. Think of potential areas of disagreement you may have with school officials regarding the IEP and develop plans to address those problems.

    a. Identify the data in the records and elsewhere supporting your position.
    b. Identify the data in the records and elsewhere supporting the school's position.
    c. Identify reasons to counter the school's position.
    d. Develop alternative proposals for achieving your goals and objectives for your child which school officials might more readily accept.
    e. Determine before the IEP meeting the minimum program you will accept for your child before appealing the IEP.

11. Determine the role you will assume during the meeting.

    a. Very assertive role, taking charge of the meeting early and guiding it. If you choose a very assertive role, a way to ensure that your own agenda is covered is to have it carefully written out and even rehearsed with your spouse or others who are there to support your point of view. Provide a copy of your agenda for each member of the IEP team to guide the meeting in the directions you wish.
    b. Assertive role, in which you allow school officials to lead the meeting but you ensure that all items on your agenda are covered completely to your satisfaction.
    c. Less assertive role, in which you allow school officials to lead the meeting and you only press for a few specified items.

12. Get another person to attend the meeting with you. Discuss with him prior to the meeting what you hope to do in the meeting and what you want him to do.

Considerations
During the IEP Meeting

1. If school officials are working with your child for the first time, initiate efforts at the first of the IEP meeting to make your child's presence felt in that meeting , as previously suggested.

2. Ensure that each item required for an IEP is fully discussed. These include:

a. a statement of your child's present level of educational performance *in all areas,* including movement, communications, social relations, independence, senses/perception, thinking, and learning style;

b. a statement of annual goals and short-term objectives for each of those goals;

c. a statement of the special education and related services to be provided to · meet each of the goals and objectives;

d. a statement of the extent to which the child will be able to participate in regular educational programs;

e. the projected dates for initiating services and the anticipated duration of the services; and

f. a statement of appropriate objective criteria and evaluation procedures and schedules for determining, on at least an annual basis, whether the short-term objectives are being achieved.

3. Decide who is to conduct the meeting. If you decide to let the school system guide the meeting by reviewing its recommended goals and objectives, anticipated services, and evaluation criteria for your child, you should follow their discussion by identifying how these items relate to the IEP you developed before the meeting. Where you agree with the proposed program, express your agreement and check off the item from your list. Where disagreements arise, seek to clarify their nature and try to reach an acceptable solution. If disagreements cannot be resolved immediately, make a note of those areas and indicate a desire to come back to these issues later and move on to new goals and objectives.

If you want to guide the meeting, tell the school officials you would like to review the elements of the IEP you have developed and would like them to comment on each item as it is brought up or after all items have been described. Then proceed to manage areas of agreement and disagreement as mentioned above.

4. As the meeting progresses, do not let participants get distracted from the IEP task itself. All participants' attention should be addressed to the elements of the IEP. Do not let the discussion wander off to unrelated matters.

5. As the discussion comes to an end, review the agenda of concerns you developed prior to the meeting. Make certain that all items in your agenda have been covered. This is a good point at which to discuss with whomever came with

you to the meeting what matters remain to be covered. If you had earlier disagreements over certain items, return to those matters and seek to resolve them.

6. At the conclusion of the meeting if you are satisfied that the IEP meets your child's needs to the fullest extent possible, you may at this time signify agreement by signing the IEP or the permission for placement document, whichever your school system requires. If, however, you want to examine the IEP without time pressure, tell the school officials you would like to review the IEP over the next day or two. Request that they provide you with a copy and tell them exactly when you will give them your final decision regarding the program and placement on the IEP. And if you do not accept portions of the IEP, identify clearly to the school officials those portions that you find unacceptable. If they will not change those items, tell them you want additional time to consider the IEP. Ask them to give you a copy, and tell them exactly when you will make your final decision.

7. Final checklist to review before signing the IEP or permission for placement document.

a. Does the IEP accurately and fully describe your child's present level of educational performance in all relevant and important areas? Does it accurately portray your child's learning style?

b. Do the annual goals describe in positive terms what skills your child will accomplish within a year?

c. Are annual goals written to build on your child's present level of educational performance?

d. Is there at least one annual goal and short-term objective for each related service your child will receive?

e. Are goals and objectives written as positive, measurable statements?

f. Do goals and objectives contain the five essential parts of *who* will do *what, how, where,* and *when?*

g. Do the annual goals and short-term objectives meet the priorities you have established as essential for your child?

h. Are all special education and related services clearly identified along with projected dates for initiating services and the anticipated duration of the services?

i. Does the IEP clearly describe the extent to which your child will be able to participate in regular educational programs?

j. Does the IEP include appropriate and understandable criteria and evaluation procedures and schedules for determining, at least on an annual basis, whether the short-term instructional objectives are being achieved?

k. If the persons to provide the IEP services are known, have you talked with those persons and ensured that they agree with the IEP and will provide these services? (If these persons attend the IEP meeting, they will have already answered these questions. If they did not attend the meeting, you should talk with them before signing the IEP.)

1. If you do not find the IEP totally acceptable, decide which of the following actions you will take:

- Sign the IEP or permission for placement document but note which parts of the IEP you find objectionable and indicate in writing your plan to appeal those parts. (This option should allow your child to get the services indicated pending appeal of the part you object to.)
- Refuse to sign the IEP or permission for placement document and indicate in writing your intention to appeal the IEP. (Before doing this, inquire as to what educational services your child will receive if this option is followed.)
- Sign the IEP or permission for placement document and indicate which parts you disagree with but write nothing about a plan to appeal. This option at least puts you on record as feeling that the IEP does not adequately meet your child's needs.

VISITING PLACEMENT OPTIONS

Before you agree to a classroom placement for your child's special education program, you will want to visit the school. Occasionally there is more than one classroom within the school system appropriate to meet the goals and objectives and to provide the support services outlined for your child. In the same way you offered unique, valuable knowledge of your child as you met with educators for evaluation, eligibility, and the IEP, you will have particular insight into the kind of environment suited to his particular learning style. By visiting school classrooms, talking to administrators and teachers, eating lunch in the lunchroom, and observing playground activities, you can assess the educational program with the needs of your child in mind. You will be able to ask questions and perhaps offer ideas to the teacher for ways in which your child can be accommodated in the classroom.

Many parents feel uncertain when they visit schools. They wonder what to look for as they observe the school program. The following outline serves as a guide for your observations. This guide will be useful as you visit a school before you give permission for your child to be placed there. It will also be valuable for those times when you have the opportunity to observe your child in his classroom after placement.

A classroom environment is structured around many components. The outline provides you with questions to ask and things to look for as you observe the many activities, materials, methods, and the physical arrangement of the classroom. You will find the outline a useful guide as you attend parent-teacher conferences.

I. Classroom organization
  A. Physical environment
    1. Layout
      a. How is furniture arranged?
      b. Are there large open areas or is the room divided into smaller components?
      c. Is the size of the furniture consistent with the size of the students? Is there any special equipment (i.e., chairs with arm supports, individual carrels, balance stools, bathroom fixtures at appropriate levels, etc.)?
      d. Where is the classroom located in relationship to the cafeteria? To the bathroom? To outdoor areas? To the special services?
    2. General atmosphere
    Is the general atmosphere relaxed or businesslike? Social or individual? Soothing or stimulating?
  B. Daily schedule
    1. Transitions
      a. What is the daily schedule? Do children seem to understand the schedule?
      b. Are support services scheduled at times that do not interrupt a child's participation in the ongoing school work?
      c. How does the teacher indicate that one activity is over and another beginning?
    2. Consistency
    Is the schedule generally the same every day?
    3. Active/quiet
      a. Does the daily schedule include active times and quiet times?
      b. Is there provision for daily outdoor activity?
      c. How frequently does the teacher change the pace?
  C. Social environment
    1. Peer interactions
      a. Are children allowed to interact spontaneously with one another? When? How often?
      b. Does the teacher facilitate constructive interactions? During school work activities? During free time?
    2. Teacher-child interactions
      a. How does the teacher relate to the children?
      b. Does the teacher tolerate and adjust to individual children?
      c. Does the teacher enter into conversations or play situations with children?
    3. Values
    What are some of the values held by the teacher and the children? Success? Creativity? Social manners? Enthusiasm? Docility? Physical prowess? Similarities? Differences?
II. Curriculum
  A. Goals and priorities
    1. What developmental areas are included in the curriculum (i.e., move-

ment, communications, relationships with others, independence/self-concept, thinking skills, etc.)?
2. What areas receive emphasis in the classroom? What is *not* a curriculum priority?
B. Materials
  1. Are the teaching materials concrete or abstract?
  2. Are the teaching materials appropriate to the developmental level of the children?
  3. Do the materials teach through various senses—vision, touch, hearing? Through movement?
  4. Are the materials accessible to children?
  5. Are the materials designed to interest children?
C. Methods
  1. Groupings
     a. Do children work individually, in small groups, or as a total class?
     b. Are the children grouped homogeneously (all at the same skill level) or heterogeneously (different skill levels in the same group)?
     c. Are the groupings different for different curriculum areas?
  2. Teaching style
     a. Is the teacher directive or nondirective in leading learning exercises?
     b. Does the teacher work individually with children or does she focus more on groups?
     c. Performance expectations
        (1) Does the teacher expect all children to perform at approximately the same level?
        (2) Does the teacher expect children to wait for their turns, or to volunteer answers spontaneously?
        (3) Does the teacher expect children to listen to and follow group verbal instructions?
        (4) Does the teacher expect children to work independently? Without interrupting with questions for the teacher?

CONCLUSION

You have negotiated the special education maze from referral through the intervening stages to a placement in a special education classroom. If this journey has resulted in educational services for your child appropriate to his needs and in the least restrictive environment, your next step involves periodic checking up on his progress. Is your child moving toward those milestones you set as goals and objectives? Are the special supportive services being given to him in the type and amount agreed upon? Is he having the time in the regular education classroom in tutoring, in the lunchroom, with children who are not handicapped?

But, you might ask, how can I know these things? Suggestions for monitoring your child's special education program are found in Chapter 8 "Checkpoints."

If at any point along the way of the maze, however, a significant and seemingly unresolvable conflict or disagreement has occurred between you and school officials, your state and federal laws provide a way for you to challenge the school system. Opportunity for a hearing before an impartial third party, a hearing officer, is provided by every school system. In the following chapter you will be assisted in weighing the pros and cons involved in deciding to go to a due process hearing.

Chapter 7

The Due Process Hearing

Detours

INTRODUCTION

In undertaking the activities described in the preceding chapters, many instances may occur in which reasonable—or unreasonable—persons disagree. Certainly there will be occasions when you find yourself disagreeing with observations, conclusions, and recommendations school officials have made concerning your child's education. And undoubtedly school officials will sometimes not concur with ideas you have about your child. When these situations arise, how are they to be mediated? Does the school system have its way by default? Must you seek appointment or election to the school board to exercise enough influence to have your way? Fortunately, a procedure known as the due process hearing exists to resolve differences that develop as you negotiate the special education maze.

Educational advocacy for special children has its legislative foundation in the Education for All Handicapped Children Act, passed in 1975 and since passed in similar form by most state governments. It provides the broad guidelines for local schools to follow in providing special education services. While state and local laws and regulations may be more detailed in their provisions than PL 94-142, those provisions cannot conflict with the federal law—at least not legally. For this reason, primary attention will be focused in this chapter on the due process hearing as described in the federal law. Should you have to use this process, however, you will need to obtain, read, and understand the specific procedures followed by your state and local school jurisdiction.

PL 94-142 not only describes the due process hearing procedure for resolving conflicts in obtaining special education for your child, but also identifies the specific conflicts that may be resolved by this process. You may initiate the due process appeal procedure *only* when you believe the school system has not fulfilled a duty it is required to perform under the law itself. Just what are these duties PL 94-142 requires of school systems?

First, they must provide a *free, appropriate public education* for all handicapped children aged three (in some states younger) through twenty-one.* The education is to be provided completely at public expense.

Second, they must ensure that handicapped and nonhandicapped children are educated together to the maximum extent appropriate. Handicapped children are to be placed in special classes or separate schools "only when the nature and severity of the handicap is such that education in regular classes," even if supported with supplementary aids or services, cannot be achieved satisfactorily. This is the legal provision mandating the education of handicapped children in the *"least restrictive environment."*

Third, school systems must *document the elements of the appropriate education* in the IEP developed by school officials and parents and described in Chapter 6.

From the school's perspective, all of the preceding three items are duties the law requires them to perform. From the child's and parents' perspectives, these are rights PL 94-142 gives to them. To guarantee that these rights are exercised, the law outlines further duties for school systems and rights for children and parents.

---

*If state law prohibits or does not authorize the expenditure of public funds to educate nonhandicapped children aged three through five or eighteen through twenty-one, a free, appropriate public education is only required for children ages six through seventeen.

Fourth, school systems must give reasonable *written notice* to parents before they evaluate or place a child, or change his special education placement, or refuse to take such actions. The notice must contain a full explanation for the school system's decision and be communicated to the parents in a manner they can understand—appropriate native language, read to them if they cannot read, and so forth.

Fifth, they must *obtain parental consent* before an evaluation is conducted, before placement is made on the basis of an IEP, before a reevaluation is done, and before any changes in eligibility or placement are made. (Procedures do exist for school systems to use to evaluate children and to provide them with special education services even if parents object. Actions of this nature, however, seldom are taken by school systems.)

Sixth, they must *provide an evaluation of the child, using a multidisciplinary team,* including at least one teacher or other specialist knowledgeable in the area of the suspected disability. A child's handicapping condition cannot be determined solely on the grounds of one test or the observations of one professional.

Seventh, school systems must *ensure that evaluation tests are nondiscriminatory.* Tests and other evaluation material must be free of cultural bias. They must reflect accurately the child's aptitude or achievement level and not be biased by the child's impaired sensory, manual, or speaking skills or other handicapping conditions. A brief explanation of the tests to be used and the information they provide must be made available to the parent.

Eighth, school systems must *make available to parents for inspection and review all records* used in the evaluation, placement, and IEP processes and those records that are a part of the child's official school file. These records must be maintained in strict confidentiality. (See Chapter 4 for a complete discussion of your rights regarding school records.)

Ninth, they must provide for the child to have an *independent evaluation* paid at public expense when (1) the parent disagrees with the evaluation results obtained by the school system; and (2) the school system agrees to such an evaluation *or* a due process hearing finds that the results of the evaluation by the school system are in fact inappropriate. These independent evaluations are usually performed by the local city, county, or state department of health or mental health services.

Finally, school systems must provide parents with an impartial due process hearing when they believe that any of the preceding rights have been violated. (The one exception is conflicts concerning school records that do not require an impartial due process hearing. See Chapter 4.) The hearing must be conducted by the state educational agency or the public agency directly responsible for the education of your child, as determined by state statute, regulation, or written policy of the state education agency.

When you believe the school system has violated any of the preceding rights of you or your child and you have been unable to resolve your differences informally, you can initiate a formal due process hearing. Remember, this process is not available to settle all disputes—only those arising from rights and duties provided in the federal law as outlined above or as set forth in your own state and local laws.

Examples of Conflicts Resolved
in Due Process Hearings

1. Whether a child should be identified as learning disabled or emotionally disturbed (evaluation/eligibility).
2. Whether a child should receive speech therapy for one or two hours per week (appropriate services and IEP).
3. Whether a child should be placed in a self-contained classroom or a regular classroom with support services (least restrictive environment).
4. Whether a child should be placed at public expense in a private school for emotionally disturbed children or should be placed in a public school program for emotionally disturbed children (appropriate education and least restrictive environment).
5. Whether the Stanford-Binet intelligence test discriminates against young, nonverbal children (nondiscriminatory testing and the need for an independent evaluation).
6. Whether a child is educably mentally retarded or trainably mentally retarded (evaluation/eligibility).
7. Whether or not a child is eligible to receive learning disability special education services (evaluation/eligibility).
8. Whether a child is receiving the program outlined in the IEP (appropriate education/IEP).

As you can readily see, each of the preceding conflicts centers upon some aspect of the child's right to a free, appropriate public education, outlined by an IEP and provided in the least restrictive environment. These represent the vast majority of conflicts brought to due process hearings. These are the areas most crucial in determining the educational progress your child will make. At the same time, decisions regarding these matters are ones where professionals may well disagree and where school systems may be forced to spend additional money if their opinions are not upheld. If you go to a hearing the chances are quite good that it will concern issues of this nature.

Seldom are due process hearings required to force school systems to perform the procedural duties of providing notice of proposed actions, obtaining parental consent for testing, offering appropriate evaluations, or allowing parents to review their child's records. Usually schools have formalized procedures for meeting these requirements. They develop form letters for notifying parents of actions they take or propose to take and for obtaining parental consent when necessary. They normally use teams for educational evaluation and try to avoid biased evaluation methods and tests. And they usually provide opportunities for parents to see records and obtain independent evaluations when they disagree with the results of the school's evaluation. Nevertheless, occasions do arise when schools do not fulfill their obligations in these matters; and if and when such occasions occur, remember your right to have a due process hearing.

CONFLICTS NOT RESOLVABLE
THROUGH DUE PROCESS

As you engage in planning your child's educational program, instances of disagreement will develop that you think should be settled in a due process hearing. You believe that your position is reasonable and that the school's position is unreasonable or wrong. You are certain an impartial third person would see the situation your way. Unfortunately, the due process hearing cannot be employed under all these circumstances. The process is only available for resolving disputes pertaining to the matters described in the previous section.

Examples of Conflicts
Not Resolved Through Due Process Hearings
   1. You desire to be at the meeting where the decision will be made on your child's eligibility for special services, and the state law does not require your presence at that meeting.
   2. You want your special child to have a particular teacher, but school officials say there are many teachers having his or her qualifications (and they are correct).
   3. You want the teacher to use a specific approach to teaching your learning disabled child how to read, but the teacher uses another approach having equal support as to its effectiveness from other professionals.
   4. In working with school officials you feel that their behavior toward you is condescending and sometimes abrasive. Although you have mentioned this to them, they continue with this behavior.
   5. You want your child moved to another class because he has a personality conflict with the teacher, but the school will not approve the change.
   6. You feel that school officials could move faster in placing your child, but they always use the maximum number of days legally allowed in making their decisions.
   7. You dislike the school psychologist who will do your child's evaluation and would like another psychologist to do the testing. The school says no change can be made without violating the time guidelines set by the law. (But you can go to a hearing on the results of these tests.)

In each of these examples the conflict relates to matters where the school system has discretion in making decisions or where the law does not require the school system to perform a specific duty. In these situations parents need to initiate informal negotiations with school officials or political action with the local school board, PTA, or other groups. Due process hearings are unavailable for resolving issues of this nature.

WHAT HAPPENS
AT THE DUE PROCESS HEARING

The purpose of the due process hearing is to allow an impartial third party, the *hearing officer,* to examine the issues upon which you and the school system disagree and to settle the dispute by making an unbiased decision. Hearing officers are usually appointed by the state educational agencies and often are lawyers, educators, or other professionals familiar with special education. The hearing officer cannot be an employee of a public agency involved in the education or care of the child, nor can that person have a professional or personal interest that could conflict with his or her objectivity in the hearing. Each state maintains a list of persons who may serve as hearing officers.

PL 94-142 does not describe in great detail the procedures to be followed in due process hearings. Most states, therefore, have developed these procedures more fully in their own laws, regulations, and policies. Numerous differences may occur from state to state regarding matters such as the degree of formality followed in the hearing; whether the hearing officer is a lawyer, educator, or other professional; whether the hearing is conducted by one hearing officer or a panel of hearing officers; and whether or not witnesses are allowed to hear the testimony of one another. Regardless of these differences, however, the basic outlines of a hearing can be described along with certain rights parents may exercise during the hearing.

RIGHTS OF PARENTS
IN THE HEARING

Although to this point the discussion has only examined when parents can initiate due process hearings, you should know that school officials can also use this procedure to resolve conflicts with parents. When parents refuse to have children evaluated or placed in a special education program, school officials may initiate a hearing to force such action. This step is seldom taken by school systems, but they may exercise this right under serious circumstances.

Whichever party initiates a due process hearing, PL 94-142 gives you certain rights to employ before, during, and after the hearing.

1. To be accompanied and advised by an attorney and by individuals with special knowledge or training with respect to the problems of your child.
2. To present evidence and confront and cross-examine witnesses and to compel the attendance of school personnel as witnesses to the hearing.
3. To prohibit the introduction of any evidence at the hearing that was not disclosed to you at least five days before the hearing.
4. To obtain a written or electronic verbatim record of the hearing.
5. To obtain written findings of fact and the decision reached by the hearing officer.
6. To have the child present at the hearing.*
7. To open the hearing to the public.*

DESCRIPTION OF THE HEARING

As mentioned earlier, hearings may be formal or informal, though usually hearing officers prefer informality—especially when parents are not represented by an attorney. The participants in the hearing will be: (1) the parents, their counsel or advocate (where used), and the parents' witnesses; (2) the school system's representative, the school system's counsel (where used), and the school system's witnesses; and (3) the hearing officer. Also in attendance, but not participating, might be a court reporter (if the hearing is transcribed) and the public, if parents have requested an open hearing.

Dr. Barbara Bateman has outlined quite well the sequence of events that occurs in a typical hearing. While these vary from state to state and as a function of the formality of the proceedings, basically a hearing proceeds in the following manner.

Sequence of Events†

1. The hearing officer checks to be sure that all is ready to "go on the record," that is, the stenographer and/or recording equipment are ready.

---

*School officals also have rights 1 through 5, but only parents have rights 6 and 7.

†Barbara Bateman, *So You're Going to Hearing: Preparing for a Public Law 94-142 Due Process Hearing* (Northbrook, Ill.: Hubbard, 1980), pp. 18-20.

2. The hearing officer will open the hearing, usually stating:

   a. the nature of the matter to be heard;
   b. the time, date, and place of hearing;
   c. the names of all parties and counsel, if any, and of the hearing officer;
   d. any factual matters already agreed to by the parties; and will
   e. ask for preliminary statements by the parties.

   3. The party requesting the hearing, the plaintiff, makes the first opening statement followed by the opening statement of the other party, the defendant. Opening statements should be brief, clear, and to the point. They explain your view of the case—the issue(s), the law, and the broad outlines of the facts. The purpose of the statement is to give the hearing officer a preview and an overview of what your evidence is going to show. A good opening statement creates an impression of clarity, organization, and control.

   4. The plaintiff calls its first witness.

   5. The hearing officer swears in the witness and asks that his or her full name be stated for the record.

   6. Counsel for the plaintiff then proceeds with the questioning. If the witness can identify documents to be introduced into evidence, that will happen while the witness is on the stand. For example:

      Counsel 1: Your honor, we'd like to introduce this document, D-1. [it is numbered then, if not previously] What is this? [showing D-1 to witness]
      Witness: This is a letter I wrote to the parents on Novement 15 stating why Jane was not eligible for special education.
      Counsel: [Shows copy to other counsel]
   Hearing Officer: Any objections?
      Counsel 2: No.
   Hearing Officer: D-1 is admitted into evidence.

   7. Counsel for the defendant cross-examines and/or questions the plaintiff's witness [optional].

   8. Counsel for plaintiff again questions witness [optional].

   9. Hearing officer questions the plaintiff's witness [optional].

   10. Steps 4 through 8 are repeated for all plaintiff's witnesses, then for all defendant's witnesses.

   11. Closing statements by parties [optional]. A closing statement summarizes your case, emphasizing the strong points you have made and the weaknesses in your opponent's case. The statement, like the opening statement, is not evidence. Rather, it is your effort to organize the case for the hearing officer so he or she views it as you wish it to be viewed. Keep it brief. Everyone, even in a short hearing, tends to feel tired and drained and anxious for it to be over.

12. Hearing officer and counsel, still on the record, discuss when written arguments or briefs, if any, are to be submitted, when the decision is to be rendered, and they check that all documents are properly marked and the hearing officer has copies, and so forth.

13. Hearing officer closes hearing by announcing, "The hearing is closed."

According to PL 94-142, the local school system must ensure that within forty-five days after receipt of a request for a hearing from a parent: (1) a final decision is reached by a hearing officer, and (2) a copy of the decision is mailed to the parent. The decision of the hearing officer is final unless it is appealed to the state education agency or a party brings a civil action in court.

In practice school systems frequently fail to meet the forty-five day time limit. When parents complain of these time violations at due process hearings, most hearing officers will criticize the school officials and direct them to comply with time requirements in the future. Seldom, however, will a hearing officer render a decision in favor of a parent merely because the school system has failed to observe legally imposed time guidelines.

DECISIONS AND APPEALS

The hearing officer does not make a final decision at the time of the hearing. The length of time the hearing officer has to reach a final decision and to notify parents is specified by state law, and usually is within fifteen calender days after the hearing.

The duty of the hearing officer is to make an independent judgment either affirming what the school system has done or proposes to do, or directing school officials to take a specific action to correct a mistake they have made. The outcome of the hearing is a clarification by the hearing officer of the rights and duties of children, parents, and school officials as to exactly what must be done in order to meet the requirements of the law. The decision must include findings of fact determined at the hearing and the recommendation of the hearing officer concerning the specific resolution of the conflict. This decision is final unless either party chooses to appeal.

If you, or the school system as well, do not agree with the hearing officer's decision, you may appeal for another hearing with the state education agency, known in many states as the State Board of Education. Each state requires such appeals to be made within a specified period, often ten to fifteen days after the initial decision. You need, therefore, to check your own state regulations to clarify this time limit.

The review made by the state education agency will also be an impartial due process hearing. The official conducting this review will examine the record developed in the first hearing to identify the substance of the issues and to see that all procedures followed due process requirements. The reviewing officer may, at his or her discretion, provide the parents and the school system the opportunity to present additional oral or written argument, or both. Finally, the official may request a hearing to obtain additional evidence believed essential to render a fair decision. A formal hearing at this appeal may not be necessary, however, when the reviewing officer believes that sufficient evidence to decide the case has been provided in the original hearing. The decision of this official is final unless you or the school system bring a civil action in court.

Should you (or the school system) believe that the decision of the state education agency is incorrect, PL 94-142 gives you the right to sue the school system in either the appropriate state court or in a federal district court of the United States. If you bring such a suit, the court will receive and examine the records of the prior hearings; will hear additional evidence at your request or that of the school system; will base its decision on a preponderance of the evidence (meaning the side having more than 50 percent of the evidence in its favor); and will direct the losing party to do whatever is believed appropriate to remedy the existing problem. Since courts are heavily burdened already, legal action of this nature may take far too long to serve as a practical remedy for problems you may face with school officials.

THINK TWICE (OR MORE) BEFORE REQUESTING A HEARING

The decision to resolve your differences with the school system through a due process hearing should not be taken lightly. Ultimately such a step will involve significant time, thought, and physical and emotional energy from both you and school officials. Probably the best definition of when you should seek a due process hearing is at the point where you feel that your back is to the wall and the only way around the impasse is a hearing. Before you reach this point, use every possible means to resolve disagreements. Attend meetings; request conferences; and listen to and seriously consider all proposed solutions. Ask questions. And provide all the information you have to prove that your view or recommendation is correct. An intermediate step, prior to the hearing, may also be advisable. This is the administrative review or conciliatory conference.

If you wish, you can skip the steps of working with the principal or special education director or attending a conciliatory conference and go directly to a due process appeal. The danger with this action, however, is that the school system may use it against you as evidence of noncooperation. Furthermore, most hearing officers and judges believe that parents should follow all possible means for resolving their problems before coming to them. So for the sake of your child's education, you need to work as closely as possible with the teachers, principal, and other administrative officials of your school system.

If you reach an impasse with your school officials, most school systems provide for an administrative review or conciliatory conference to resolve troublesome issues before going to a hearing. Usually one or more persons are brought in as neutral third parties to hear the issues and to find an acceptable solution. These third parties are most often drawn from the ranks of schoolteachers and administrators not directly involved in the problem. Since these third parties are employees of the school system, many parents do not feel that a fair solution can be reached in these meetings. Experience with such conferences, however, suggests that acceptable solutions frequently are developed when parents and school officials work in good faith.

The procedures followed by administrative reviews or conciliatory conferences are outlined in state and local laws and regulations. The authority of such committees varies. In some states the conciliatory conference committee can make binding decisions for the school system. In others the committee functions solely as a mediator attempting to help parents and school officials find an agreeable solution to their problems. Once again, you will need to examine your own state and local laws to determine the functions of this committee in your school jurisdiction.

In deciding whether to use the intermediate step of a conciliatory conference prior to requesting a hearing, one consideration in particular is important. Have you already discussed your problem with top-level school administrators, and have they stated their position on your problem? If high-ranking administrators have already advised you of their position on your problem, a conciliatory conference will probably have little value for you. Since the conference committee is headed by school employees, it will be unlikely to make decisions contrary to positions already taken by their superiors. In short, the conciliatory conference may be very useful when higher school administrators have not already considered your case. But when those administrators have passed prior judgment on the issues you are raising, it probably should be bypassed completely.

FACTORS TO CONSIDER AND WEIGH
BEFORE REQUESTING AN APPEAL

The decision to request a due process appeal affecting your child's special education program is a serious matter. If you request an appeal, both you and school system officials will expend significant time, energy, and money before the appeal is finally decided. For this reason, you should consider carefully and thoroughly each of the following matters.

First, do you understand clearly the position of the school system regarding the education of your child, and do you know what evidence—facts, reports, professional testimony—they will present to support their position? Without this knowledge, you will be unable to determine what you are appealing, your chance of winning an appeal, and, ultimately, whether or not you should request an appeal.

Second, are you absolutely clear as to what you believe is wrong with the school system's actions or decisions? Do you possess or can you obtain evidence demonstrating that the school's actions or decisions are incorrect? Unless you can articulate precisely where and why the school system is in error, you will be unable to gather evidence to support your case. Furthermore, unless you can submit evidence at the hearing to prove the school's error, the hearing officer cannot rule in your favor.

Third, do you know exactly what services, placement, or other actions you believe the school system should take to provide your child with a free, appropriate public education in the least restrictive environment? Can you obtain evidence to support these educational recommendations for your child? Hearing officers are often not educators. Therefore, it is not enough for you merely to show that what the school system is proposing is inappropriate. You will also need to convince the hearing officer of the correctness of your own educational recommendations. This requires additional research and evidence gathering.

Fourth, when you look at the evidence supporting your position and weigh it against the evidence supporting the school's position, which is more convincing? If the evidence for both positions is equally persuasive, the hearing officer will usually give the educational professionals the benefit of the doubt. Unless the evidence is well over 50 percent in your favor, you will have a very, very difficult case to win.

Fifth, where will your child be placed during the time required to process the appeal? Normally, your child will remain in the existing placement pending the outcome of the appeal. If you like where your child is currently placed and the school is recommending a placement you do not like, you may want to appeal merely to keep your child where he or she is until a resolution of your disagreement is obtained. But what if you do not like your child's current placement but still want to continue with the appeal?

If you wish to place your child in a private school pending the outcome of the appeal, you should first obtain written agreement for such action from the school officials. If the private placement is upheld by the hearing officer, the school system will be directed to reimburse you. If you move your child without permission by the schools, however, you will probably receive no reimbursement even if you win the case. Likewise, if you move your child to a private school, with or without the school's concurrence, and your appeal is not upheld, you will have to pay the private-school expenses yourself.

If you do not like your child's current placement, you may find there is no alternative to leaving him or her in that placement until the appeal is complete. Once the hearing officer announces a decision, the school system will place your child in the educational situation required by that decision—either the situation you proposed, the situation proposed by the schools, or yet a third alternative designed by the hearing officer.

A sixth factor to consider is whether you want a lawyer or educational advocate to represent you at the hearing. If you hire an attorney you should anticipate paying anywhere from $500 up, win or lose. An advocate will also usually cost something. Many lawyers will accept such cases on a pro bono (free) basis. Or you may be eligible to obtain a lawyer from your local legal aid office or a federal or state legal corporation office. Wherever you obtain counsel, you should anticipate spending many, many hours with them in preparing and presenting your case. In addition, extra expenses may well be required to acquire professional witnesses such as doctors and educational diagnosticians.

A decision to go to a hearing is a commitment of substantial time, money, and psychic energy. Above all, *parents should not go to a hearing unless they both are in agreement that such action should be taken.* Preparing for and participating in a hearing requires the cooperation and support of both parents. If you do not both agree a hearing is the only route to go, you will probably not weather the hearing process very well.

The final factor to consider before requesting a due process appeal is the benefits that will occur if you win your case. The most important benefit, of course, is that your child will receive an appropriate educational program designed to meet his or her specific developmental and educational needs. You could even put a dollar value on the benefit by examining how much a similar program would cost—if you could get it—from a private school. A second benefit is that you will have saved your child from the harm that might have accompanied an inappropriate educational program. For example, the school system might have diagnosed your child as emotionally disturbed rather than learning disabled. If the school is wrong and is proven so on appeal, the benefit you receive is saving your child from the inaccurate "label," seriously emotionally disturbed.

Once you have examined the potential costs and benefits of an appeal and have weighed the chances of winning your case, you are ready to make a final decision. If the potential benefits are greater than the potential costs, you may well want to go to an appeal. If the potential benefits and costs are about equal, you may want to consider alternative ways to provide your child with what you believe is an appropriate educational program, such as obtaining private placement or services at your own expense. If the costs are much greater than the potential benefits, you will have to decide if you can afford those costs should you lose the appeal.

The decision to request a due process hearing is not an easy one to make. By examining each of the preceding matters, you can understand more completely the implications of your choices and have greater confidence in the correctness of your final decision. One last suggestion—once you have considered these matters, discuss them with friends, professionals and others familiar with your situation. You will be amazed at how often these persons will see potential costs and benefits of your choices that you have overlooked.

CONCLUDING OBSERVATIONS

The impartial due process hearing has promoted the objectives of the Education for All Handicapped Children Act in two important respects. First, the existence of this process has put school officials on notice that their actions may be reviewed by impartial third parties if parents feel that mistakes have been made. The awareness of such a review has caused school officials to become more careful, discreet, objective, and open in their work with special children and their parents. Without the cloud of the due process hearing hanging over their heads, many school systems might lapse into the practices of prior years when the attitude seemed to be that the educational professionals know what is best and parents are merely pains to be ignored or eliminated by taking aspirin.

The second way due process hearings have advanced the goals of PL 94–142 is by actually correcting mistakes made by school systems. Considering the hundreds and thousands of special children school systems must serve each year, it is little wonder that mistakes are made. These mistakes, however, need not go uncorrected today. As parents learn of their children's and their own due process rights, they can use these rights as another mechanism for enhancing their educational advocacy skills and influence. This chapter has sought to inform you of how and when to use the due process hearing. In the final analysis, the due process hearing should be a last resort for correcting mistakes made by school systems. But because the due process hearing exists for parents to use, its use is needed less often. That is as it should be.

Chapter 8

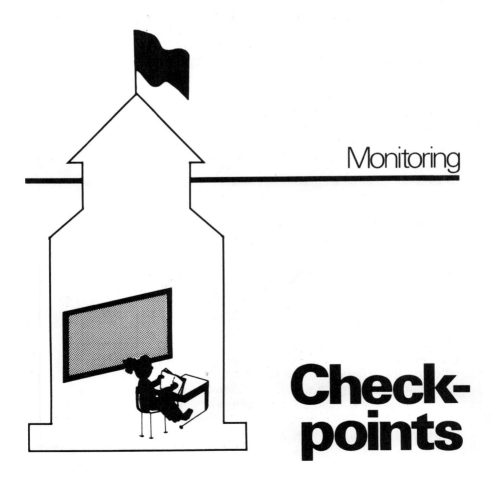

Monitoring

Check-
points

WHY MONITOR?

You have traveled a long way since first entering the special education maze. Referral, evaluation, and eligibility determination seem like dim shadows. Even decisions regarding placement and the IEP are less clear than the day they were made. But now your child is in the appropriate classroom, with appropriate services *scheduled* to be given. The maze is completed!

Wait—not so fast!

All activities you have engaged in so far have been essential in the preparation for the journey. But your task is not completed! Placing a child in a class, establishing educational goals and objectives, and scheduling services on an IEP are not the same as achieving those goals and objectives and delivering those services. The maze is only completed when your child begins to realize his or her potential as a result of a free, appropriate public education in the least restrictive environment. The maze is only completed when you monitor your child's IEP and the educational and developmental growth derived from the learning program spelled out in that document.

But why, you ask, must I monitor my child's program and progress under the IEP? Can't I trust the school system to live up to what they say will be done? Doesn't there come a time when you have to turn the educational reins over to the "experts"? And isn't now that time?

Yes, most school systems can be trusted to implement the IEP they develop for your child. Nevertheless, attempts to implement the IEP may fall short for numerous reasons: a lack of funds to hire occupational therapists, a teacher falling ill for several months, a sudden increase in enrollment leaving less time to work with your child. These and other factors may result in your child's IEP not being implemented. *And they are not legitimate reasons for failing to implement the IEP.* If you know the IEP is not being carried out, you may immediately intervene to get it back on track. But if you have not monitored the IEP, you may find yourself in the position of Mr. and Mrs. Boswell.

The Boswells' son, Billy Bob, had a major speech handicap. The IEP for Billy, therefore, included individual speech therapy, twice a week, for thirty minutes each period. As the year progressed the Boswells saw little advancement in their son's speech skills. Nevertheless, they kept hoping progress would come, in time. At the end of the school year the Boswells met with Billy's teacher, Mrs. Prizer. During their conference, Mrs. Prizer proudly showed Mr. and Mrs. Boswell Billy Bob's language board. The board contained letters of the alphabet, simple signs for frequently used words—I, go, open, close, and other communication symbols. Mrs. Prizer explained that Billy Bob would carry this small board around his neck throughout the day. When he wanted to communicate with someone, he would point to the appropriate symbols on his board. The Boswells were impressed with this innovation, although somewhat surprised they had not learned of it before the end of school. When they asked Mrs. Prizer how the board was used with Billy Bob's speech therapy, they learned of yet another innovation in their son's IEP. "Oh," said Mrs. Prizer, "Billy Bob has not had speech therapy for seven months. When he showed no progress after two months of therapy, we decided to use the language board as an alternative to speech therapy to improve his communication skills."

Maybe the language board was more useful than speech therapy, but that is not the point. No change in the IEP should be made without your consent. Without monitoring your child's IEP, you won't know that innovations are being made in your child's program. Yes, once the IEP is completed you can turn the educational reins over to the "experts." But you should continue to monitor the education and developmental directions in which those reins are leading your child.

Most parents approach the topic of monitoring the IEP with fear and trepidation. They wonder, "Who am I to question what the educators are doing?" "How will I know whether the IEP is being implemented?" "What do I do if the IEP is not being followed?" Combine this uncertainty with the normal tendency to trust "authorities," and no wonder parents become timid at the thought of second-guessing school officials and teachers.

What can you do to overcome these understandable common fears? Your first concern should be to focus on special aspects of the IEP to determine (1) if the educational plan is in fact being implemented, and (2) if the plan is working well for your child. Four more questions you might ask are:

1. Is the classroom instruction following the IEP?
2. Is my child receiving the special services indicated?
3. Is the classroom setting truly appropriate for my child's needs?
4. Is my child making educational and/or developmental progress in school?

Having identified the questions to ask for effective monitoring, your second concern becomes finding the answers to those questions. What techniques are available to find the answers to these questions? Parents have found many techniques to be helpful when monitoring their child's IEP. The most frequently used methods include the following:

CONFERENCES   Individual meetings with your child's teachers, school administrators, tutors, therapists, and other professionals.

CLASSROOM OBSERVATION   Visits to the classroom with the specific intent of observing some aspect of your child's learning activities. Volunteering in the class and at the school and using those opportunities to observe your child and his or her program.

NOTEBOOKS   Sent between you and your child's teacher in which you share comments, suggestions, observations, and the like. Also included can be a checklist of important behavioral goals and objectives from the IEP.

GROUPS   Active participation in your local Parent-Teacher Association and in local parent groups such as the Association for Children with Learning Disabilities and the Autistic Society. These groups often provide excellent up-to-date information on programs and school services relevant to your child's IEP.

YOUR OWN CHILD   Ask your child how school is going; what are the most enjoyable activities in school; how much time does he or she spend in speech or math. Look over his homework, what he has to do and has done. Help him or her with homework.

These are but a few of the techniques you might use to assess your child's program and progress during the school year. While the list is not complete, it provides a starting point from which you can begin to develop your own monitoring plan.

YOU AND YOUR CHILD'S TEACHER

The single most important source of information on your child's progress is his or her teacher. The teacher talks with you after school, at the IEP meeting, and at regularly scheduled conferences. The teacher completes your child's report card and fills out the notebook you send back and forth. The teacher talks with the school psychologist, the physical therapist, and administrators; and then the teacher talks to you.

The free flow of information between you and your child's teacher will depend mostly upon the relationship existing between the two of you. If the teacher perceives you as a concerned parent who also understands the needs and problems of teachers, you will probably receive plenty of up-to-date, specific information about your child's progress. But how do you as a parent develop this cooperative relationship with your child's teacher?

Many parents have found the following suggestions to be helpful.

1. Try to develop a personal relationship with your child's teacher. Some families feel comfortable inviting their child's teacher to dinner; others find regular telephone conversations helpful.
2. Give the teachers/specialists sufficient time to know your child before asking their opinions about his or her progress, problems, the appropriateness of program, and so forth.

3. Obtain general information on the routine objectives and procedures of the classroom (when does math come; when is recess scheduled; what books are being used?) before visiting the class.

4. Respect the teacher's routines and fit your observations within them when visiting the class.

5. Tell the teachers/specialists what you like about their teaching style—they'll be pleasantly surprised you noticed.

6. Convey to the teachers/specialists your understanding of the difficulties they frequently face in doing their job—be empathetic to their needs, too!

7. Prepare for conferences in advance by developing and bringing with you a list of questions, concerns, and comments. This saves everybody time.

8. Communicate to teachers/specialists what is important to *you* in the education and development of your child.

9. Share your plan for monitoring your child's IEP, and follow through with that plan.

10. Discuss problems with the teachers/specialists you believe have arisen in implementing the IEP. Don't begin by going right to the school administrators.

11. Consider ways you might volunteer time or materials for the classroom.

Each of the preceding activities offers an excellent occasion for you to build bridges of trust and openness with teachers and other specialists working with your child. As these relationships are developed and strengthened, you will experience more and more confidence in your ability to know and understand your child's progress, and the extent to which the IEP is actually being implemented.

OBSERVING IN THE CLASSROOM

Besides communication with the teacher, another exceptional source of information for monitoring your child's educational progress is classroom observation. Schools vary in how receptive they are to allowing parents' observation of classroom activities. How receptive teachers are to parent classroom visits also differs (another good reason for developing an open relationship with the teacher). In all cases, however, before you visit your child's classroom, check first with the teacher and then the school principal to determine the specific policy in your area.

Once you know the school policy on classroom visits, you are ready to prepare yourself for this monitoring activity. Following are several suggestions designed to increase the effectiveness of your classroom visit.

1. Give the teacher sufficient prior notice of your visit.
2. Decide what you want to observe (e.g., reading group, playground time) and then let the teacher know your plans.
3. Tell the teacher specifically how long you plan to spend in the classroom.
4. Observe only your own child or interactions involving your child and other children or adults.
5. Keep your conversations with professionals or other adults to a minimum during your observation time.
6. After the classroom visit make some notes describing your observations, impressions, high points, low points, and/or concerns.
7. Follow up your observation with a brief conference (or phone call or note) sharing your findings, thoughts, and questions with the teacher.

Whenever you go for a classroom visit remember that many people, teachers included, can be uncomfortable in situations where they are being observed. The tension created by not knowing why you have come to observe can cause unnecessary anxiety, and even real misunderstanding between you and the teacher. Notifying the teacher of your desire to observe your child, explaining the purpose of your visit, and following up after the observation can relieve much potential tension. These steps should smooth the way for a productive classroom observation and open relationship with your child's teacher.

BEING AN INFORMED CONSUMER

Being an informed consumer is also helpful in your monitoring efforts. Although you are not expected to be a special educator, physical therapist, or other

special education professional, you can still learn many basic ideas important for monitoring the education of your child. For example, you can learn about current teaching methods and therapeutic techniques as they relate to your child's disabilities. This information can be obtained in many ways: from parent groups and associations that conduct workshops; from classes and special lectures or presentations; from individual professionals who are willing to share their knowledge with parents; from the local PTA; from attending continuing education

library

classes on topics of special education presented by local community colleges and universities; and from books, pamphlets, and magazines. In these and many other ways, you can become a knowledgeable consumer of the special education services in your local school system. And as an informed consumer you will also become an effective monitor of your child's educational program and progress.

SUMMING UP

Monitoring the IEP is hard work. Only time, energy, and careful thought can make it pay off. The jargon found in many IEP's, "educationese," is often impossible to decipher. Educators know what they mean by voice quality or voice intensity, for example, but parents may not. Make certain, therefore, to ask questions at the time of the IEP conference so you *do* know what the IEP means as well as what it says. This is basic to effective monitoring.

Knowing if the goals and objectives are appropriate can cause difficulties also. Your own sense of your child helps you here. Strengthening Exercises # 1 through # 3 described in Chapter 2 will give you the added confidence to evaluate the annual goals and short-term objectives suggested for your child's IEP. Monitoring by checking up on the dates of the short-term objectives can help you further in assessing the continuing appropriateness of goals and objectives. Are the objectives being met on schedule; ahead of schedule; not at all? Answers to these questions will lead you to others. If the results are positive or negative, what accounts for those results? Is it the program? The teacher? The classroom setting? The answers to all these questions may require some changes in your child's IEP.

MAKING CHANGES

What happens when your monitoring activities lead you to decide change is necessary? Where do you start the change process?

making changes

Elements of the IEP can be changed at any time through mutual agreement of the IEP team. But once you have agreed to an IEP, you should wait a reasonable time before deciding the program is or is not working, and seeking changes.

What is a reasonable time? In part this depends upon your child's developmental speed and the educational skills being taught. Where your child naturally develops slowly or the educational skill requires significant time to acquire, three to five months may be necessary before noticeable progress occurs. Where development is rapid and the skill more readily learned, you may feel that changes should begin to take place within one to three months. In either case, a useful approach would be to wait until the time for assessing achievement of the initial short-term objectives. If these objectives are clearly not being met, a change in program, services, teachers, or some combination of all three may be in order.

The preceding diagram of circles suggests that the best place to begin your change efforts is with your child's teacher or other specialists. If problems are resolved at this initial level, changes will often be immediate and on target. At this first level of change, the process for correcting problems is the least complicated—although it may not seem so. If your efforts to alter the IEP are unsuccessful at this level, you move out one circle toward the perimeter and seek change at the administrative level.

As discussed in an earlier chapter, efforts to work with school administrators to make changes in your child's IEP should initially be made informally. An informal request for an IEP change will often be all that is needed. The request should be accompanied by an explanation and monitoring data supporting reasons for the request. Should this fail to be sufficient, you can then initiate the formal administrative review procedures available in most school systems.

When satisfactory results are unattainable through the administrative process, your next step is to request a due process hearing. As pointed out in Chapter 7, you must consider this step very carefully before deciding whether to take it. In some instances, however, no alternative actions may be available. Therefore, even though several months may pass before a final ruling is made to change your child's IEP, the due process hearing remains a viable method for achieving potential change. Of course, if the due process proceedings all seem futile or their results still seem biased and inaccurate, changes in the IEP can also be sought through court action. Considering the time and cost involved in this action, however, its use should probably be reserved only for those major IEP disagreements concerned with private school or residential placement, or the provision of support services where none are currently provided.

Where, then, does the last circle on the perimeter—political and legal advocacy—enter the IEP change process? This outer circle usually is activated to force school systems to do something they currently are not doing—for example, providing physical therapy or psychological counseling services—or to do better and more extensively things they are doing on a limited scale—for example, vocational training, speech therapy. In both instances, parents work singly and jointly to pressure school administrators, school boards, city councils, and state legislators to appropriate additional funds for these activities. Or parents sue in court to force school jurisdictions, and indirectly legislative bodies, to abide by the law and to provide appropriate services. Through either activity the results may be the same—the child receives the program and/or services in the kind and amount appropriate to meet his or her educational needs.

As the change process moves further from the center of the circle, the importance of the child's needs sometimes becomes less and less the focus. Change activities taken by teachers are usually made rapidly, with up-to-date information, and in an understanding environment. Where IEP changes are generated at points further from the child, the decisions may be slow in coming, out of date, and made out of context. Again, this speaks to the need for close relationships with the teacher. Begin and end with the teacher whenever you can. You will be miles ahead.

During the school year your child's teacher or other school officials may come to feel that your child's progress is not satisfactory. When this occurs they usually will notify you, seeking additional information or even suggesting a conference. In some instances they may even request formal evaluations of your child. If this happens the material you read on evaluation procedures in Chapter 3 will once again become relevant to negotiating the special education maze.

Generally, however, school systems have too few resources to evaluate your child each year. Thus, their formal monitoring process, involving extensive psychological, educational, and other evaluations, usually occurs only every three years. This is the school's triennial evaluation.

The practical results of the triennial evaluation are many. First, this usually means that your child will be placed in a particular program and left there for three years, unless something extraordinary happens, or unless you personally request a change. Second, since no formal evaluations will probably be done for three more years, the only monitoring of your child's progress will be done by the teacher, by other professionals working with your child, and by you. Since even conscientious teachers and other school professionals have limited time to provide services, they often devote little effort to monitoring the results of their work. Therefore, if you don't monitor your child's IEP carefully, three years could go by only to discover that little or no progress has occurred. Your child cannot afford that time.

Finally, every three years you will be faced with a new eligibility determination decision. Pressures on school systems are growing to cut the costs of special education. This may lead them to deny services completely to children who are mildly handicapped; to provide resource programs to children who need self-contained programs; or to place children in special day-school programs when an appropriate education requires residential placement. In the face of these pressures, you must be prepared to present a clear, convincing case as to what, for your child, is an appropriate education in the least restrictive environment. By monitoring your child's IEP carefully and consistently and by following the steps outlined earlier in this book, you should be well on the road to presenting that compelling case for your child each time the triennial evaluation rolls around.

Chapter 9

Does the Maze Ever End?

A REVIEW
OF THE SPECIAL EDUCATION MAZE

For years parents have been confused, frustrated, and generally perplexed in their attempts to understand how school officials make decisions about the education of their special children. As parents talk with teachers and administrators and hear of evaluation and eligibility procedures, IEPs, learning disabilities, ITPA test scores, and due process hearings, they often feel that schools have built a complex special education maze through which only educators can find the way. Parents frequently have not known how to take the first step toward negotiating this maze.

This book has been written for parents—and their special children. In the preceding pages parents were introduced to the corridors of the special education maze—the circular process of referral, evaluation, eligibility, IEP, placement, monitoring, and, when necessary, due process procedures. By understanding this process, you will have gained insight on where to enter the maze, the rules and regulations for traveling through the maze, and potential strategies. The end result of your efforts, it is to be hoped, will be that your special child receives a free, appropriate public education in the least restrictive environment.

Emphasis throughout this book is placed upon the importance of parents acquiring the skills, knowledge, and values essential for becoming effective educational advocates for their special children. Federal and state laws have created the legal basis for ensuring that handicapped children receive a free, appropriate public education. Local school systems, and their teachers and administrators, have the potential knowledge, dedication, and resources to implement these laws. You, as parents, however, possess the one additional ingredient needed to blend these laws and resources together for the effective education of your child. This ingredient is your precise, unique, and loving knowledge of your child, what he knows and how he learns. If this knowledge is not included in educational planning and programming for your child, the program ultimately developed will be incomplete, possibly inappropriate, and conceivably ineffective. Your child cannot afford to lose days, months, and years in such a program. You do not want this time to be lost, or you would not be reading this book.

Educational advocacy promises a means for parents to participate actively, intelligently, and cooperatively in decisions affecting the education of their special children. Educational advocacy offers you an approach for ensuring that your special knowledge of your child is reflected in the educational program, the teaching methods, and the educational environment your child encounters. Educational advocacy provides parents with a plan of action for successfully negotiating the special education maze.

A NEW EXPERIENCE
WITH EACH TRIP THROUGH THE MAZE

The special education planning and programming cycle, described in Chapter 1, is a recurring one. Each year the educational goals, objectives, and services outlined in your child's IEP are reexamined, updated, and revised as needed. For many parents, the planning cycle—the maze—need be negotiated but once. After a year of special education services, their children overcome or compensate for their disabilities and return to the regular classroom. For most parents, however, the maze will be traveled many times. But no matter how frequently parents go through the maze, they must remember that each trip is in fact a new one.

Each trip, whether it is the annual review or the more extensive triennial reevaluation, will see changes in the key people, that is, the parents, the child, and school officials; shifts in the laws, regulations, and policies pertaining to special education; and, often, alterations in the strategies used by school officials to implement the rules of the maze. The fact that each trip through the maze is a new experience has significant implications for parent educational advocates.

First, as the cycle begins again, parents must gather new data on their child; analyze the data; organize it for purposes of making evaluation, eligibility, IEP, and/or placement decisions; and prepare for and participate in the meetings where these decisions are made. All of this, of course, will be more easily accomplished when the child's program has been carefully monitored by the parents.

Second, since laws, regulations, policies, and practices change rapidly in this field, parents should check annually with their state and local education agencies for any changes in these procedures that may have occurred since they last traveled the maze. By following this suggestion you will in effect be editing this guide for parents year by year.

Third, because school personnel come and go as frequently as rules and regulations change, you should also continually update the key people chart found earlier in this book. By asking around you should be able to learn something about the educational and experiential background of these "new people." Only by keeping your information up to date can you hope to negotiate with the educators in the special education maze with confidence and trust.

Fourth, each year brings new problems and opportunities to local school systems. These problems and opportunities often are translated into budgetary terms and then into program implications—frequently fewer services, higher student/teacher ratios, and longer bus rides. These problems and opportunities will sometimes change the strategies used by school officials to fulfill what they perceive as their duties for educating handicapped children in accordance with federal and state law. By knowing the particular problems and opportunities confronting your school system, you will be better prepared to face any changes in strategy school officials may seek to implement.

Finally, since each trip through the maze is a new one, you will have to formulate new strategies and tactics to be sure they meet the changed conditions. Past success in obtaining an appropriate education for your child indicates that you planned and implemented well that journey through the maze; but past success does not promise continued success. Only thoughtful, careful, hard work can prepare you to be an effective educational advocate for your child. There is no substitute for diligent preparation for negotiating the maze.

The special education planning cycle and the rules and regulations governing the implementation of that cycle are established by federal and state laws and by the rules, regulations, policies, and practices of state and local education agencies. You may find that no matter how skilled you become in negotiating the special education maze, your child's program never seems appropriate to meet his or her needs. Classes may be too large, related services unavailable, self-contained classrooms nonexistent, and transportation inconvenient. When these problems arise and due process procedures, short of court action, fail to correct them, educational advocacy has reached its limits of effectiveness. Legal and political advocacy must then be employed to bring about necessary changes.

Legal advocacy is required when school officials interpret the law one way and you another. Although in due process hearings, hearing officers may agree with the interpretations of school officials, their word is not final. Only the courts can give a definitive answer. Courts define the meaning of federal and state laws, courts rule authoritatively on whether state and local education policies and regulations conform with federal and state laws. When you feel that state laws concerning the education of special children conflict with federal laws, and school officials will not change the maze to meet your objections, the courts offer one alternative for changing both the system itself and the policies and regulations governing it.

Yet another option for altering the special education system is political advocacy. This alternative encompasses the efforts of groups who specifically lobby legislative, executive, and administrative bodies in an attempt to change government budgets, policies, and procedures. The distinguishing feature of political advocacy is its emphasis upon changing specific elements of the special education maze, e.g., procedures for evaluation, criteria for eligibility, budgets appropriated for special education, and certain rules for special education, such

as the number of days in which IEPs must be completed and the rights of parents
to participate in various meetings. In contrast to educational advocacy, where
the advocate is concerned only with the welfare of one child, political advocacy
seeks changes in the overall process and the encompassing rules and regulations
in order to benefit all special children. This type of advocacy may be essential
when the process itself is flawed or where the rules and regulations are inherently
unjust or impractical. In these situations educational advocacy will prove insufficient and nothing short of political advocacy will assure a free, appropriate
public education for special needs children.

Legal and political advocacy have their place, but their effects often are
felt only in the long run. In the short run your child needs immediate services
and educational programs that meet his or her unique needs. Educational advocacy, as outlined in the preceding pages, is designed to assist you in meeting
these short-run educational needs. As parents gain skill and experience in using
legal, political, and educational advocacy, they will increasingly learn the situations in which each is most effectively employed—and will use them accordingly.
But in the last analysis, when the special education system and accompanying
regulations have been altered by legal and political advocacy, success in negotiating the newly designed system will ultimately depend upon parents' competen-
cies to serve as educational advocates for their own children.

THROUGH THE MAZE WITH OTHERS

At many points in the special education planning cycle you have been encour-
aged to have a friend assist and accompany you in your role of educational
advocate. This was true in evaluation, eligibility, IEP/placement, and due process
proceedings. The purpose of this suggestion is at least twofold. First, another
person may serve as the source of ideas, suggestions, and "a second pair of eyes
and ears" to enhance your effectiveness as an educational advocate. Second,
another person can provide the personal and emotional support most parents

need when engaging in the stressful activity of traveling through the special education maze. As others provide these supportive contributions, you will find them an essential ingredient to effective educational advocacy for your child.

While the help and assistance of one or two friends is a necessity for effective educational advocacy, the combined efforts and support of numerous other parents will tend to enhance even further the effectiveness of your advocacy activities. By creating a team of parents committed to becoming educational advocates for their children, you will immediately experience an increase in knowledge about the nature of your own local school maze and a decrease in the debilitating feeling that you are alone in learning to cope with the techniques and frustrations of negotiating that maze. A few coalitions of parents currently exist in certain areas of the nation; a list of them is found in Appendix C.

The experience of the Parent Educational Advocacy Training Center in Alexandria, Virginia, has shown just how effective parent groups in educational advocacy can become. Since 1978, the training center has trained hundreds of parents to serve as educational advocates for their children. These parents came together in groups of fifteen to thirty for fifteen hours of training focused upon the ideas discussed in this book. From this training course parents acquired insights into the special education process in their local school jurisdictions, skills in educational advocacy to work within that process, and a sense of identity and solidarity with other parents of handicapped children.

Upon leaving the course, graduates took with them the names of other parents upon whom they could call as they initiated their educational advocacy efforts. A survey of these "graduates" revealed that large numbers have in fact drawn upon one another's insights, knowledge, and experience. In addition, these parents have received from one another the frequently needed psychological and moral support necessary to sustain them as they traveled through the maze. As these parents have gained proficiency as educational advocates, often they have reached out to help other parents who have not attended the Parent Educational Advocacy Course. These examples of mutual support and assistance represent the very best parents can do to ensure the responsiveness of the system to their special children.

How do you start your own group of educational advocates? A good place to begin is by having a number of concerned parents, not more than fifteen to twenty, study this book as a group. If you can enlist the assistance of special education teachers, school psychologists, or other professionals who work with handicapped children, they may provide the group with expertise to explore certain selected topics, e.g., evaluation, eligibility, IEPs, or due process procedures, more intensely. But remember, this book was meant for you—the parent. Don't let the professionals take over *your course.* The intent of the group study is to make you an effective educational advocate for your child. Any professional assistance you get should be oriented toward helping you transmit your unique insights of your child into his or her special educational plans and programs.

Conveying unique understandings of your child to schoolteachers and administrators and monitoring your child's educational program are tasks only you, as a parent, can perform. Unless you consciously and actively fulfill the role of educational advocate for your child, the promise of the Education for All Handicapped Children Act will never be realized. Unless parents throughout the country join together to learn the knowledge, skills, and values of educational advocacy, they will continue to be ill prepared to fulfill their crucial responsibilities as partners with school officials in making educational decisions for their special children.

The promise of the law can be made a reality. The partnership of parents and school officials can profitably be established. Why not ensure these things occur by organizing parents to become educational advocates in your community?

Appendices

Divisions of Special Education in the United States

Exceptional Children & Youth
State Dept. of Education
868 State Office Bldg.
Montgomery, AL 36130
(205) 832-3230

Exceptional Children & Youth
State Dept. of Education
Pouch F
Juneau, AK 99811
(907) 465-2970

Div. of Special Education
State Dept. of Education
Pago Pago, Am. Samoa 96799
(9-0) 633-4789

Div. of Instructional Services
State Dept. of Education
1535 W. Jefferson
Phoenix, AZ 85007
(602) 255-3183

Div. of Instructional Services
State Dept. of Education
Arch Ford Education Bldg.
Little Rock, AR 72201
(501) 371-2161

Special Education Division
Dept. of Public Instruction
721 Capitol Mall, Rm. 614
Sacramento, CA 95814
(916) 445-4036

Pupil Services Unit
State Dept. of Education
201 E. Colfax
State Office Bldg.
Denver, CO 80203
(303) 866-2727

Bureau of Pupil Personnel & Special Ed.
  Services
State Dept. of Education
P. O. Box 2219
Hartford, CT 06115
(203) 566-4383

Special Programs Division
Dept. of Public Instruction
Townsend Bldg.
Dover, DE 19901
(302) 736-5471

Div. of Special Ed. Program
State Dept. of Education
10th & H Streets, N.W.
Washington, DC 20001
(202) 724-4018

Bureau of Education for Exceptional
  Students
State Dept. of Education
319 Knott Bldg.
Tallahassee, FL 32304
(904) 488-1570

Prog. for Exceptional Children
State Dept. of Education
State Office Bldg.
Atlanta, GA 30334
(404) 656-2678

Special Education Section
Dept. of Education
P. O. Box DE
Agana, Guam 96910
(9-0) 772-8300

Special Needs Branch
State Dept. of Education
1270 Queen Emma St., Rm. 1201
Honolulu, HI 96813
(808) 548-6923

Special Education Division
State Dept. of Education
650 W. State St.
Boise, ID 83720
(208) 334-3940

Dept. of Special Ed. Services
Illinois Office of Education
100 N. First St.
Springfield, IL 62777
(217) 782-6601

Div. of Special Education
Dept. of Public Instruction
229 State House
Indianapolis, IN 46204
(317) 927-0216

Div. of Special Education
Dept. of Public Instruction
Grimes State Office Bldg.
Des Moines, IA 50319
(515) 281-3176

Div. of Special Education
State Dept. of Education
120 E. 10th St.
Topeka, KS 66612
(913) 296-3866

Bureau of Education for Exceptional
  Children
State Dept. of Education
Capitol Plaza Tower, 8th Floor
Frankfort, KY 40610
(502) 564-4970

Special Education Services
State Dept. of Education
Capitol Station, Box 44064
Baton Route, LA 70804
(504) 342-3631

Div. of Special Education
State Dept. of Educational & Cultural
  Services
State House Complex
Augusta, ME 04333
(207) 289-3451

Office of Special Education
Office of Education, TTPI
P. O. Box 24 CHRB
Capital Hill
Saipan, CM 96950
9870/9319 (overseas operator)

Div. of Special Education
State Dept. of Education
200 W. Baltimore St.
Baltimore, MD 21201
(301) 659-2489

Div. of Special Education
State Dept. of Education
31 St. James Ave.
Boston, MA 02116
(617) 727-6217

Special Education Services
State Dept. of Education
P. O. Box 2008
Lansing, MI 48902
(517) 373-1695

Special Education Section
State Dept. of Education
Capitol Square Bldg.
550 Cedar St.
St. Paul, MN 55101
(612) 296-4163

Special Education Section
State Dept. of Education
P. O. Box 771
Jackson, MS 39205
(601) 354-6950

Div. of Special Education
Dept. of Elementary and Secondary
  Education
P. O. Box 480
Jefferson City, MO 65101
(314) 751-2965

Special Education Unit
Office of Public Instruction
State Capitol
Helena, MT 59601
(406) 449-5660

Special Education Section
State Dept. of Education
Box 94987, Centennial Mall
Lincoln, NE 68509
(402) 471-2471

Div. of Special Education
440 W. King St.
Carson City, NV 89701
(702) 885-5700

Special Education Division
State Dept. of Education
105 Loudon Rd., Bldg. #3
Concord, NH 03301
(603) 271-3741

Special Education & Pupil Personnel
  Services
State Dept. of Education
225 W. State St.
Trenton, NJ 08625
(609) 984-4955

Div. of Special Education
State Dept. of Education
300 Don Gaspar Ave.
Santa Fe, NM 87503
(505) 827-2793

Office of Education for Children with
  Handicapping Conditions
State Dept. of Education
Education Bldg., Rm. 1073
Albany, NY 12234
(518) 474-5548

Div. of Exceptional Children
Dept. of Public Instruction
Raleigh, NC 27611
(919) 733-3921

Special Education Division
Dept. of Public Instruction
State Capitol
Bismarck, ND 58505
(701) 224-2277

Div. of Special Education
State Dept. of Education
933 High St.
Worthington, OH 43085
(614) 466-2650

Sec. for Exceptional Children
State Dept. of Education
2500 N. Lincoln, Suite 263
Oklahoma City, OK 73105
(405) 521-3351

Div. of Special Education
State Dept. of Education
700 Parkway Plaza
Church St.
Salem, OR 97301
(503) 378-3598

Bureau of Special and Compensatory
  Education
P. O. Box 911
Harrisburg, PA 17126
(717) 783-6913

Special Education Program for Handicapped
  Children
Dept. of Education
Box 759
Hato Rey, PR 00919
(809) 764-8059

Special Education Unit
State Dept. of Education
235 Promenade St.
Providence, RI 02908
(401) 277-3505

Office of Prog. for Handicapped
State Dept. of Education
Rm. 309, Rutledge Bldg.
Columbia, SC 29201
(803) 758-7432

Section for Special Education
Div. of Elementary and Secondary
  Education
New State Office Bldg.
Pierre, SD 57501
(605) 773-3678

Education for the Handicapped
State Dept. of Education
103 Cordell Hull Bldg.
Nashville, TN 37219
(615) 741-2851

Div. of Special Education
Texas Education Agency
201 E. 11th St.
Austin, TX 78701
(512) 475-3501

Special Education Programs
Utah State Board of Education
250 E. 5th South
Salt Lake City, UT 84111
(801) 533-5982

Special Education & Pupil Personnel
  Services
State Dept. of Education
120 State St.
Montpelier, VT 05602
(802) 828-3141

Div. of Special Education
Dept. of Education
P. O. Box I
Christensted, St. Croix
Virgin Islands 00820
(809) 773-1095

Div. of Special Education
State Dept. of Education
P. O. Box 6Q
Richmond, VA 23216
(804) 225-2065

Dept. of Public Instruction
7510 Armstrong St., S.W.
Tumwater, WA 98504
(206) 753-2563

Div. of Special Education
State Dept. of Education
Capitol Complex, Rm B-057
Charleston, WV 25305
(304) 348-2034

Div. for Handicapped Children
GEF III, 4th Floor, B 93
125 S. Webster
Madison, WI 53702
(608) 266-1649

Office of Exceptional Children
State Dept. of Education
Hathaway Bldg.
Cheyenne, WY 82002
(307) 777-6215

BIA, Dept. of the Interior
Dept. of Exceptional Children
Code 507, 18th & C St., NW
Washington, DC 20240
(202) 343-5517

Educational Planning Chart: The Process in Several "Languages"

PARENTS	VIRGINIA	MASSACHUSETTS	WISCONSIN	MARYLAND	NEW YORK	CALIFORNIA	YOUR STATE
Awareness	Referral (local screening committee)	Referral	Referral	Referral	Referral	Referral	
Information Gathering	Evaluation by a multi-disciplinary team	TEAM (evaluation team)	M-TEAM	Admission, Review, Dismissal Committee	Committee on the Handicapped, Phase I	School Appraisal Team/ Educational Assessment Service	
Acceptance	Eligibility Committee						
Planning	IEP Meeting	TEAM Meeting	M-TEAM Plan		Committee on the Handicapped, Phase II. IEP Planning Conference	IEP (written by SAT/ EAS)	
Programming Checking Up	Placement Annual review, also triennial reevaluation	Placement Review ten months after initial placement in special ed. Triennial reevaluation	Placement Annual review Triennial reevaluation	Placement Review initial placement in sixty days Annual review Triennial reevaluation	Placement Annual review Triennial reevaluation	Placement Annual review Triennial reevaluation	

Parent and Consumer Organizations for Handicapped Children

American Alliance for Health, P.E. and
 Recreation
1900 Association Drive
Reston, VA 22901

American Athletic Association of the Deaf
3916 Lantern Drive
Silver Spring, MD 20902

American Association of Mental Deficiency
5101 Wisconsin Avenue, NW
Washington, DC 20016

American Deafness and Rehabilitation
 Association, Inc.
814 Thayer Avenue
Silver Spring, MD 20910

American Occupational Therapy
 Association
1383 Piccard Drive
Gaithersburg, MD 20760

American Orthotic and Prosthetic
 Association
1444 N St., NW
Washington, DC 20005

American Physical Therapy Association
1156 15th St., NW
Washington, DC 20005

American Speech and Hearing Association
1801 Rockville Pike
Rockville, MD 20852

National Association of Sports for Cerebral
 Palsy
P. O. Box 3874
Amity Station
New Haven, CT 06525

National Association for the Deaf-Blind
2703 Forest Oak Circle
Norman, OK 73070

National Easter Seal Society for Crippled
 Children and Adults
2023 W. Ogden Avenue
Chicago, IL 60612

National Therapeutic Recreation Society
1601 N. Kent Street
Arlington, VA 22209

National Organizations

ALL DISABILITIES
American Coalition of Citizens with
 Disabilities
1346 Connecticut Avenue, NW
Washington, DC 20006

The Information Center for Handicapped
 Individuals, Inc.
120 C Street, NW
Washington, DC 20001

AUTISM
National Society for Autistic Children
169 Tampa Avenue
Albany, NY 12208

BLIND

American Council for the Blind
1211 Connecticut Avenue, NW
Washington, DC 20006

American Foundation for the Blind
15 West 16th Street
New York, NY 10011

National Federation of the Blind
1346 Connecticut Avenue, NW
Suite 212, Dupont Circle Building
Washington, DC 20036

CEREBRAL PALSY
American Academy for Cerebral Palsy and
 Developmental Medicine
P. O. Box 11083
2405 Westwood Avenue
Richmond, VA 23230

United Cerebral Palsy Association
66 East 34th Street
New York, NY 10016

DEAF

Alexander Graham Bell Association for the
Deaf
3416 Volta Place, NW
Washington, DC 20007

International Association of Parents of the
Deaf (IAPD)
814 Thayer Avenue
Silver Spring, MD 20910

National Association of the Deaf
814 Thayer Avenue
Silver Spring, MD 20910

DEAF-BLIND

National Association for the Deaf-Blind
2703 Forest Oak Circle
Norman, OK 73071

EMOTIONALLY DISTURBED

American Association of Psychiatric
Services for Children
1725 K Street, NW, Suite 1112
Washington, DC 20006

Mental Health Association, National
Headquarters
1800 North Kent Street
Arlington, VA 22209

EPILEPSY

Epilepsy Foundation of America
1828 L Street, NW, Suite 405
Washington, DC 20036

LEARNING DISABILITIES

National Association for Children with
Learning Disabilities
4156 Library Road
Pittsburg, PA 15234

MENTAL RETARDATION

American Association of University
Affiliated Programs for the
Developmentally Disabled
2033 M Street, NW, Suite 406
Washington, DC 20036

Joseph P. Kennedy, Jr., Foundation
1701 K Street, NW, Suite 205
Washington, DC 20006

National Association for Down's Syndrome
P. O. Box 63
Oak Park, IL 60303

National Association for Retarded Citizens
2709 Avenue E East
P. O. Box 6109
Arlington, TX 96011

National Down's Syndrome Congress
528 Ashland Avenue
River Forest, IL 60305

Special Olympics, Inc.
1701 K Street NW, Suite 203
Washington, DC 20006

PHYSICALLY HANDICAPPED

National Easter Seal Society for Crippled
Children & Adults
2023 W. Ogden Avenue
Chicago, IL 60612

National Paraplegia Foundation
333 North Michigan Avenue
Chicago, IL 60601

National Center for a Barrier Free
Environment
1140 Connecticut Avenue, NW, Room 1006
Washington, DC 20036

Spina Bifida Association of America
343 South Dearborn, Room 319
Chicago, IL 60604

SPEECH IMPAIRED

American Speech and Hearing Association
10801 Rockville Pike
Rockville, MD 20852

NATIONAL ADVOCACY ORGANIZATIONS

Center for Law and Education
Guttman Library
6 Appian Way
Cambridge, MA 02138

Center on Human Policy
216 Ostrom Avenue
Syracuse, NY 13210

Children's Defense Fund
1520 New Hampshire Avenue, NW
Washington, DC 20036

Closer Look Information Center for the
  Handicapped
P. O. Box 1492
Washington, DC 20013

Council for Exceptional Children
1920 Association Drive
Reston, VA 22091

Mental Health Law Project
1220 19th St., NW
Washington, DC 20036

Mexican-American Legal Defense Fund
28 Geary Street
San Francisco, CA 94108

National Association for the Deaf
Legal Defense Fund
Florida Avenue & 7th St., NE, Suite 311
Washington, DC 20002

National Center for Law and the
  Handicapped
1235 North Eddy Street
South Bend, IN 46617

National Juvenile Law Center
St. Louis University School of Law
3701 Lindell Boulevard
St. Louis, MO 63108

Native American Rights Fund
1506 Broadway
Boulder, CO 80302

Parent Coalition Projects

Parent coalitions included in this list have received funds from the Special Education Programs of the U.S. Department of Education. The coalitions are made up of a broad spectrum of parents' groups whose purpose is to train parents. The training encompasses the rights parents and their handicapped children have under Public Law 94-142 and the ways they can exercise those rights to assure that their children receive a free, appropriate public education. The intent is not adversarial, but a trained, knowledgeable group that works with the schools and other related service agencies to assure appropriate programming for handicapped children.

Parents Educating Parents
Georgia Association for Retarded Citizens
1851 Ram Runway, Suite 104
College Park, GA 30337
(404) 942-5270

Coordinating Council for Handicapped
  Children
407 S. Dearborn Street, Room 680
Chicago, IL 60605
(312) 939-3513

Task Force on Education for the
  Handicapped
812 E. Jefferson Boulevard
South Bend, IN 46617
(219) 234-7101

New Hampshire Coalition for Handicapped
  Citizens, Inc.
P. O. Box 1422
Concord, NH 03301
(603) 224-7005

Southwest Ohio Coalition for Handicapped
  Children
3024 Burnet Avenue
Cincinnati, OH 45219
(513) 861-2400

Parent Educational Advocacy Training
  Center
228 S. Pitt Street, Room 300
Alexandria, VA 22314
(703) 836-2953

Designs for Change
220 South State Street
Suite 1616
Chicago, IL 60604
(312) 922-0317

PACER (Parent Advocacy Coalition for
  Educational Rights)
4701 Chicago Avenue South
Minneapolis, MN 55407
(612) 827-2966

Governor's Advocacy Council for Persons
  with Disabilities
116 W. Jones Street
Raleigh, NC 27611
(919) 733-3111

PEP Coalition (Parent Education Project)
United Cerebral Palsy of Southeastern
  Wisconsin, Inc.
Suite 434
152 W. Wisconsin Avenue
Milwaukee, WI 53203
(414) 272-4500

Southern Nevada Association for the
  Handicapped
1918 Pinto Lane
Las Vegas, NV 89106
(702) 384-8122

PAVE (Parents Advocating Vocational
  Education)
1516 North Orchard
Tacoma, WA 98406
(206) 752-5354

Parents' Campaign for Handicapped
  Children and Youth (Closer Look) and
  the Council for Exceptional Children
1201 16th Street, NW
Washington, DC 20036
(202) 822-7900

Federation for Children with Special Needs
312 Stuart Street, 2nd floor
Boston, MA 02116
(617) 482-2915

Federal Agencies and Congressional Offices

United States Senate Subcommittee on the
  Handicapped
Room 10-B
Russell Senate Office Building
Washington, DC 20510

United States House of Representatives—
  Subcommittee on Select Education
320 Cannon House Office Building
Washington, DC 20515

Special Education Programs
400 6th Street, SW
Donohoe Building
Washington, DC 20201

Developmental Disabilities Office
Office of Human Development
330 C Street, SW
Room 3070
Washington, DC 20201

Office of Handicapped Individuals
Office of Human Development
200 Independence Avenue, SW
Room 338D
Washington, DC 20201

President's Committee on Employment of
  the Handicapped
1111 20th Street, NW
Washington, DC 20210

President's Committee on Mental
  Retardation
7th & D Streets, SW, Room 4025
Washington, DC 20201

Index

PARENT EDUCATIONAL ADVOCACY TRAINING CENTER
228 South Pitt Street, Room 300
Alexandria, Virginia 22314

PLEASE SEND ME INFORMATION ON:

☐   How to arrange for a Parent Training Course in Educational
     Advocacy in my district

☐   How to form a team to participate in the Parent/Professional
     Team training program to learn how to present the Parent
     Training Course in my district

NAME:_____

POSITION:_____

ADDRESS:_____

_____
           city   state   zip

TELEPHONE:__(___)___-_____